EARS TO HEAR

Hearing God's voice correctly by way of the cross

EARS TO HEAR

Hearing God's voice correctly by way of the cross

Timothy & Carla Williams

Published by WinePress Publishing, PO Box 428, Enumclaw, WA 98022.

ISBN 1-57921-718-4
Library of Congress Catalog Card Number: 2003111752

Dedicated to our sons, Joshua and Josiah who listened for God's voice as to whom they should take as wives. May they always have ears to hear that they may be a Bride for Christ.

> The Spirit and the bride say, "Come!" And let him who hears say, "Come!" Whoever is thirsty, let him come; and whoever wishes, let him take the free gift of the water of life. (Revelation 22:17)

Contents

Foreword

As a child I wanted to hear God's voice more than anything in the world. On Sunday, my family sang songs about God that said, "We walk and talk as good friends should and do," or "He walks with me and he talks with me and tells me I am his own." I longed for my voice to "ring with laughter" with God's. But sadly our denomination didn't believe that God divinely interacted with us today. So when I asked my father, an elder and lay minister, how to hear God, he told me the words of another song that said He lived "beyond the azure blue" and that the "prophets of old heard His voice" but now He "speaks from His inspired word."

God's grace must have been with me because I persisted in my desire to hear His voice with all my heart. At that wonderful age of twelve, the same age Jesus stayed behind at the temple, I demanded that my father explain to me why the Scriptures promise that Jesus' "sheep know" His voice. Wasn't I His little lamb? We preached that if God's word says something we believe and obey it, then why didn't we believe we could hear Him? I finally realized that my father couldn't tell me because he blocked his ears from the voice of God. Like many people, I became discouraged and disillusioned with the church.

Then one day, after many years of teenage struggle and rebellion, I realized that God had been speaking to me all along. I didn't yet understand the biblical doctrine that explained how we hear God, I just knew His voice. By this time I was married and had a child of my own, and fortunately my husband longed to know God and to hear His voice more clearly. When we prayed as a young couple for God to give us "ears to hear Your voice," we had no idea what that really meant. Looking back on that prayer I wonder if we would have asked for God's voice if we understood the cost.

After almost 30 years of striving to distinguish God's voice from our own and those of others, Tim and I have come to learn that to know His voice, we must die to ourselves. Jesus knew His Father's voice, but He only heard it clearly through suffering and denying His own voice. Many ask us, "How do you really hear God? How can you be so sure?" And we ask, "Are you willing to silence your own voice?"

This book has burned on Tim's heart for many years, but we still had lessons to learn—and we learn new ones every day. Many, young and old, ask us to teach them to hear God, and His Spirit now urges us to share what He has taught us. Tim will lay out the authority and biblical doctrine of how "the prophets of old" heard God's voice and how the Bible clearly teaches we can today. We will share how we applied these things to our own lives; the times we heard God clearly and the times not so clearly. Paul said in 1 Corinthians 10:11 that the stories of old were "written down as warnings" so that we could learn from their errors. We made a lot of mistakes along the way, but those times helped us to desire more of the cross of Christ in order to put our own voices to death. God does indeed speak through "His inspired word," but also through people, through circumstances, and directly to our hearts. It is our hope that this book will encourage you to silence all other voices and gain "ears to hear."

—CARLA WILLIAMS

Chapter 1

The Voice of God

What do we mean by the voice of God? All that the Bible denotes as the voice of God. It can mean the voice of God declared through the universe that we see around us.[1] It can be an audible voice spoken to our human ears, or the voice spoken to one's heart or soul by the Holy Spirit. God's voice can be His presence in circumstance or in the use of spiritual gifts. He may speak to us through an individual or messengers, such as angels or prophets. God's voice goes forth in many ways and He is no respecter of manner or way of speaking. He speaks on His terms and in any way He chooses and those who listen to God will know in their "spirit" that He has spoken.

> Immediately Jesus knew in his spirit that this was what they were thinking in their hearts, . . . (Mark 2:8)

In the Bible God spoke in many ways, sometimes in fire or water, or whispers or thunder, or visions or thoughts, or through the spirit or soul of man. He spoke through prophets and miracles, once through a donkey and another time with writing on a wall. Indeed, Jesus spoke in a boat, on mountainsides, and even drew in the dirt. God continues to speak today in many ways and fashions, so we should listen for His voice in any way He chooses to speak. Let us simply, with a full heart of faith, set our minds on things above so we might be privileged to hear angels singing in the far distance.[2]

The most important thing for us to realize is that we need to face the truth about every situation. The odds are stacked way against us that we will hear God correctly, that we will too easily declare, "The word of the Lord"[3] when we have not heard God at all. Our hearts are deceptive above all things.[4] Sin deafens us to the voice of God, and Satan always stands ready to twist God's Word as soon as it is spoken.

An Offensive Message

The church as a whole does not teach the offensive message of the cross that crucifies opinion. Therefore each group considers their dogma the voice of the Lord. Then there are those in church fellowship, some with good intentions, who offer advice that does not spring from enlightenment by the Holy Spirit and death to self, but from mockery the flesh can perform in the name of the Lord. Our fleshly desires and the opinions of others cloud and mislead us in directions opposite of God's will. Add to this the multitude of books, commentaries, and devotionals that speak of hearing God or entering His presence but without a resolve to know nothing but Jesus Christ and Him crucified, that only muddle the voice of God.[5]

Many think that if we read the Bible, understanding the Greek and Hebrew, we already have the voice of God. Ink on paper is not the voice of God. Besides the ink on paper, the Holy Scriptures, tells us to listen for more than a printed book. As the Bible declares, Greeks look for wisdom and Jews for miracles but we preach Jesus crucified and that is how we obtain ears that can hear. It is not with the mind of man that we understand God. Nor can we hear God by seeing miracles. Rather those who come to God with no dependance on themselves to hear Him, will hear His voice.

> Jews demand miraculous signs and Greeks look for wisdom, but we preach Christ crucified: a stumbling block to Jews and foolishness to Gentiles. (1 Corinthians 1:22–23)

We cannot just let life come at us, ask the Lord's blessing, and assume He is with us. Counting our blessings will not work either because God blesses the wicked along with the righteous. We know many in false and empty churches that still think they are right with the Lord because of all the blessings in their lives. Goodness, Jesus healed many, but in reality only a few were His sheep.

Deceptive Voices

The Gibeonite deception is a perfect example of looking at the externals of everyday life without really seeking the Lord. Joshua had defeated many of the enemies of God while marching into the Promised Land. As a result the Gibeonites feared Israel and schemed a plan to protect themselves against Joshua's army.

> "And our elders and all those living in our country said to us, 'Take provisions for your journey; go and meet them and say to them, "We are your servants; make a treaty with us."' This bread of ours was warm when we packed it at home on the day we left to come to you. But now see how dry and moldy it is. And these wineskins

> that we filled were new, but see how cracked they are. And our clothes and sandals are worn out by the very long journey." The men of Israel sampled their provisions but did not inquire of the Lord. (Joshua 9:11–14)

On the surface, everything looked correct, but Joshua failed to inquire of the Lord. Likewise we may think something is of God but we must prayerfully discern if it truly comes from Him. For example, circumstances may point to God leading us to buy a house, join a church, travel, or do something we want. Everything may point to yes, yet a trap laid down by the Evil One. Our flesh wants something and we deceive ourselves into seeing God work when He is really not in it. We may read our Bibles but God not be in the Bible reading. We may go to church and everything look and feel like God is present, but we must test, examine, and inquire to see if the Lord is really in it.

We must learn to always ask, "Where is the voice of the Lord?" The bread may be dry and moldy, the wineskins empty and cracked. The clothing may be worn and show signs of the truth, but not be of God or come from His Holy Spirit. We must make sure that our life is holy or God may allow a lying spirit to lead us to our destruction, as he did to King Ahab. For without hearing God's voice, we will always come up short and sinful in our obedience to Scripture and to God. We simply cannot be our own god speaking to ourselves the Bible and bestowing the blessings of God. We need to learn from King Saul, that we need to hear and obey the voice of the Lord above all our sacrifices, prayers, and talk.

> But Samuel replied: "Does the Lord delight in burnt offerings and sacrifices as much as in obeying the voice of the Lord? To obey is better than sacrifice, and to heed is better than the fat of rams." (1 Samuel 15:22)

Such things, and more, conspire against us to keep us from hearing God correctly. Indeed, our flesh does not want to do God's will even if we understand what He says. In fact, this book cannot touch on how to do God's will,[6] but we will see how we can obtain ears that hear, to "consider carefully how" we listen.

Therefore consider carefully how you listen . . . (Luke 8:18a)

HEARING AIDES

- How do you feel that God may have spoken to you in the past? In what ways could you have been wrong about His voice? Are you willing to face the truth that you could have heard wrong?

- What feelings arise in your heart when you hear the phrase "The offensive message of the cross"?

- List some things you feel may keep you from hearing the voice of God.

Chapter 2

The Burning Bush

Now Moses was tending the flock of Jethro his father-in-law, the priest of Midian, and he led the flock to the far side of the desert and came to Horeb, the mountain of God. There the angel of the Lord appeared to him in flames of fire from within a bush. Moses saw that though the bush was on fire it did not burn up. So Moses thought, "I will go over and see this strange sight—why the bush does not burn up." When the Lord saw that he had gone over to look, God called to him from within the bush, "Moses! Moses!" And Moses said, "Here I am." (Exodus 3:1–4)

Moses noticed the burning bush and probably thought, "I will go over and see this strange sight—and why that bush does not burn up." Stopping his work to notice the bush set up the opportunity for Moses to hear the voice of God. God took notice that Moses paid attention.

Moses was busy tending the flock, just as we bustle around in our daily lives today. The vast majority of mankind remains too busy to notice the "burning bush" that God places before them and therefore fail to ever hear Him speak.

The oddness of a burning bush unconsumed by the fire, drew Moses closer. He had no idea the holiness of God awaited him or that the angel of the Lord was in the flame.[1] Unlike Moses, most of us remain too self-absorbed to notice God's signs and perish in our sins, simply because we never bother to listen for God to speak. Indeed, many are too busy in their church work to hear God's voice.

> When Jacob awoke from his sleep, he thought, "Surely the Lord is in this place, and I was not aware of it." (Genesis 28:16)

The Desert

So it is with us. God seeks to get our attention through the things of life. As Job declares, God sends the snow and rain to stop men from their labors in hopes they will stop and listen for His voice.[2]

Just like Jacob, we sleep, totally unaware that God seeks to speak.[3] If we take the time to come out of our selves, we will discover the holiness of God and hear Him talking to us in all aspects of life.

"When the Lord saw that he had gone over to look, God called" Moses by name. Indeed, God would call Moses' name twice in the account of the burning bush showing how eagerly He wanted to talk to this man. If we would but take one step in faith to inquire when God calls, we would hear our name said twice. Most are too weighed down, as Jesus said, by dissipation[4] to even take the time to hear God's voice. And if God called our name a hundred times, we still would not stop because we have not taken the time to notice the burning bush. Our hearts stay too busy with ourselves.

To prepare ourselves to hear from God we must go to the "far side of the desert" as Moses did. Away from the world and away from our busy thoughts and plans. This is why God put John the Baptist out in the desert preaching. We must go to the desert where refreshment from the world is sparse. Most of us cannot literally herd flocks to the mountain of God in the desert, but we can enter our prayer closets and shut out the world. As Jesus said, we must close the door when we pray. We can, while in the prayer closet, silence our religious voice that uses Scripture and the name of the Lord to mock the voice of God to obtain what we want. We can take notice of the burning bushes God places before us in our daily lives and stop, listen, and wait for Him to call us to come closer.

The flaming bush burns in our hearts, souls, or in the physical situations that God places in our lives. For within the burning bush of our life situations God calls us, if we would but take notice. Like David we can go into our prayer closets and just sit before the Lord.[5]

God seeks to start the fire of holiness in your life, and you must first take notice and go over and look. You must ask yourself, "How does one hear God's voice?" and "What would it mean for my life to hear His voice?"

Faith and Obedience

Faith must be present if we want to hear God's voice. Many who claim to be Christians do not even believe that God talks to His children today, and all we need is the Bible and our minds to know the will of the Lord. As we will see, the Bible tells us we must get beyond ink on paper and hear the voice of the Lord. Moses had this faith when he heard the voice come from the bush and did not waver in unbelief. He did not run away thinking he heard something strange, or that such a thing could not happen in his day.

Immediately Moses said, "Here I am." If you doubt that God communicates on a first name basis with His children, you will never hear His voice. In fact, Jesus could not do any miracles in His hometown because of their unbelief.[6] Moses had ready faith to meet the burning bush and most importantly the second requirement—a willing heart to obey.

Though Moses was by no means perfect, the pure seeds of faith and obedience were present. God only gives the Holy Spirit to those ready to "obey Him." Do not think for a moment that God will talk to you if you are not ready to obey.

> We are witnesses of these things, and so is the Holy Spirit, whom God has given to those who obey him. (Acts 5:32)

So many do not hear God's voice, or hear it wrong, because they do not have an honest heart ready to obey. They have bought into the current gospel messages that strip obedience from faith.[7] Let us not forget that although God called Moses, He also met him on the road to kill him because something was amiss.[8]

Holy Ground

When we ask God to talk to us, we ask a very holy thing, for He is holy and His voice is holy. Moses didn't realize he stood on holy ground. Likewise we do not know how unworthy we are to hear His voice and so in our ignorance we do not know to "take off" our "sandals." Holy means to be set apart and our ears must be set apart from all other voices. Nothing man has made should stand between us and the Lord. For all that man makes, thinks, and does is tainted with sinfulness. The sandals of our church doctrine, religious thoughts, desires, or plans must not come between God and man. The sandals that take us where we want to go and the designs our own minds and hands have created should not keep us from hearing God.

We must become silent, quiet not only in words, but also in our thoughts and hearts.[9] The voice of our sinful nature must be crucified. The voice of our entertainment, stray thoughts, and understanding of Scripture must be silent. We must be careful that our prayers are not too long[10] and that by God's power we enter the Sabbath rest still reserved for us.[11] This is the work of the Holy Spirit, to crucify us to these things. Our flesh that agrees with God's will must be crushed and fully hated. When this happens we become a people of rest and peace, ready to hear the voice of God.

He is perfect and the world He created is sufficient for man. God's holiness is all a man needs. Moses learned this when he neither drank water nor ate for forty days and nights while fellowshipping with God.[12]

> "Do not come any closer," God said. "Take off your sandals, for the place where you are standing is holy ground." Then he said, "I am the God of your father, the God of Abraham, the God of Isaac and the God of Jacob." At this, Moses hid his face, because he was afraid to look at God. (Exodus 3:5–6)

Falling in Love

Later when Moses passed on the Ten Commandments and all the requirements of the Law he sought to speak to the hearts of the people. For God wants us to go beyond, law, rules, and principles. God wants us to fall in love with Him, to treasure His fellowship, to desire above all—to hear His voice. Just as no groom would want a bride to marry him just because the law said she had too, does God want us to believe in Him that way. God's desire is that two lovers, oblivious to rules, just simply fall in love with each other. To "love the Lord your God, listen to his voice and hold fast to him" because He is our very life.

> And that you may love the Lord your God, listen to his voice, and hold fast to him. For the Lord is your life, and he will give you many years in the land he swore to give to your fathers, Abraham, Isaac and Jacob. (Deuteronomy 30:20)

Are you willing to attempt the impossible? Are you willing to listen for God's voice and obey that voice in all things? Then don't come any closer until you have taken off your sandals. Before you answer, be sober, look around and consider how many claim to hear God's voice, yet you know they really do not hear Him correctly. They have ears, but they cannot hear.

Hearing Aides

- What has been your past belief about the voice of God?

- What "sandals" do you need to remove in your life in order to stand on holy ground?

- Can you think of any burning bushes that God may have brought into your life?

- Are you ready and willing to do anything to hear God clearly?

Chapter 3

The Sin of Unbelief

> The Lord would speak to Moses face to face, as a man speaks with his friend. Then Moses would return to the camp, but his young aide Joshua son of Nun did not leave the tent. (Exodus 33:11)

Moses spoke to God face and face and today we have a greater covenant than his. Therefore we should be able to say, "I speak to, and listen to God, better than Moses." But alas, how little true faith we find in the church today.

Unbelief is the inspiration of Satan and the ultimate sin of man. Men's hearts are so darkened that they can look at the stars and the planets and declare there is no God. Man cannot even hear the voice of the stars declare there is a God.[1] Man either ignores the voice or worships the stars. How blackened is the heart of man who can go to church to worship the living God but doubt that He speaks to him whom His Son died for. Men in this sickened state often read the Bible and conclude it declares God is silent today.

How often Jesus was moved by holy frustration to exclaim, "How long shall I put up with you?" Unbelief caused our Savior to desire to hurry to heaven asking those who doubted, "How long must I stay with you?"

> "O unbelieving and perverse generation," Jesus replied, "how long shall I stay with you and put up with you? Bring your son here." (Luke 9:41)

Only a perverted heart, darkened by sin's blackness, would dare test God by asking, "Does God speak to His children today?" But alas, many standing in pulpits preach that all we need is ink on paper, the Bible. And vastly more people know God speaks to His children, but have not really heard His voice. All because we are an unbelieving and perverse generation that would rather hear our own voices than the voice of our Creator.

Let us confess with the deepest of mourning and tears, that to doubt that God speaks today is the vilest of sins. Jesus flatly tells us, "My sheep listen to my voice." In many things Jesus spoke in parables, but not so when it came to hearing God's voice. Jesus clearly declared that His sheep listen for His voice and follow that voice.

> My sheep listen to my voice; I know them, and they follow me. (John 10:27)

Which Voice?

In truth, all men listen to a voice. A man either listens to the voice of God or the voice of Satan.[2] There is no middle ground. Those who do not listen for the voice of God listen to the voice of Satan.

Today the old Serpent asks, "Does God really talk to men?" just as he did in the Garden of Eden when he asked Eve, "Did God really say?" Satan caused Eve to doubt her

Creator's instructions. And today as sin increases[3] Satan continues to ask, "Does God really say?" Many in church believe that God does not talk to His sheep. Unbelief is taught as if it were faith to believe God is silent. It is darkness called light and bitter labeled sweet.[4]

Only a darkened heart and a bad conscience causes one to believe God does not talk to His children. What would you think of someone who went around telling children that their earthly father will no longer talk to them? What would you think of a parent who told a small child that his dad did not talk to him anymore? That all that dad wanted the son or daughter to do was read some letters about him and obey those letters? They would never hear their father's words of comfort or rebuke, nor feel the arms of an embrace. We would become indignant with this preacher, yet we tolerate, even embrace, Bible colleges, pastors, teachers, and denominations that live lives of unbelief and teach that listening for God's voice remains a thing of the past. That somehow now that we have the Bible, ink on paper, that God will not talk to His children. Well, let us look at what the ink on paper declares and repent of all unbelief.

> You show that you are a letter from Christ, the result of our ministry, written not with ink but with the Spirit of the living God, not on tablets of stone but on tablets of human hearts. (2 Corinthians 3:3)

The Voice of Salvation

We cannot claim salvation in Jesus Christ if we do not believe that God talks to His children. To claim the salvation of Jesus without hearing the voice of God makes someone a dead Pharisee without the hope of heaven. Such people resemble a bride who is more in love with the letters her groom sent rather than the embrace of his arms. Again, Jesus spoke clear and to the point, no one becomes a true

Christian without hearing the voice of God. No one remains saved unless they are individually "taught by God."

> No one can come to me unless the Father who sent me draws him, and I will raise him up at the last day. It is written in the Prophets: "They will all be taught by God." Everyone who listens to the Father and learns from him comes to me. (John 6:44–45)

God's voice was not just for old prophets or just for the New Testament church, but the blessing of His fellowship is for all God's sheep. "They too will listen to my voice," Jesus declared. They too, though not of the sheep pen of the Old Testament or of the first church, but of the church today, will listen for the voice of Jesus and follow the one Shepherd.

> I have other sheep that are not of this sheep pen. I must bring them also. They too will listen to my voice, and there shall be one flock and one shepherd. (John 10:16)

Children of God

Jesus told us empathetically that He did not leave us as orphans who must fend for themselves. We are not to be orphans in this world begging for some meager understanding of what God's will is for us each day.

> I will not leave you as orphans; I will come to you. Before long, the world will not see me anymore, but you will see me. Because I live, you also will live. On that day you will realize that I am in my Father, and you are in me, and I am in you. (John 14:18–20)

"On that day you will realize," Jesus said this to show the unity of the Son and the Father. They were one and their very existence, fellowship, and power were completely one. In other words, we can be just as close to God as Jesus was. We have been called to walk as Jesus walked and this fact should forever close the argument of whether God speaks to His sheep.[5] We realize that Jesus is in the Father and we in Him, so we too can gain a small taste of the fellowship Jesus had with the Father. Then we will say with John 14, because Jesus lives we "also will live."

People in the world, or the worldly in the church, cannot accept this fact. They have never heard His voice so they cannot verify that God speaks today to His children.[6] Even if the Bible were the voice of God, do we foolishly think we could take it all in and apply it? Clearly we need someone to teach us day by day, hour by hour, minute by minute, and second by second. If we don't see this, we might as well give a first grader all the books he needs and tell him to go figure it out without a teacher. But look at what the Bible declares, they had been "taught by God to love one another." He spoke to each person's heart and guided them as to how to love one another. God was their teacher, not some man, not a manual called the Bible, but the living God came and spoke to each person, empowering them and directing them in how to love each other. This is why the first church could have all things in common and stand perfectly united in thought and mind.[7]

> Now about brotherly love we do not need to write to you, for you yourselves have been taught by God to love each other. (1 Thessalonians 4:9)

If unbelief causes us to not listen for the voice of God we must first begin by repenting of this sin. Otherwise we will be lost in a sea of questions, what ifs, and speculations that only increase our fears rather than a faith that allows us to sit quietly at the feet of Jesus to listen. If we want to have ears to hear, then we must open them wide by the power of faith.

Hearing Aides

- Name some things or doctrines that cause doubts about hearing God's voice. How do these things breed unbelief?

- What does it mean to you to be a sheep that belongs to God?

- Why is it important that we hear God personally and directly?

Chapter 4

The Promised Land

It takes three things to hear God's voice correctly and have ears that hear. We will examine the third aspect toward the end of this chapter, but first we need faith and secondly an obedience that comes from that faith.[1] If obedience is absent then the faith is folly expressed in religious words and deeds. If we desire the riches of the promised land then we must rid ourselves of unbelief and cultivate a faith that obeys. To obey the Bible without belief in the voice of the Holy Spirit is to become a legalist. To claim to believe in the voice of the Lord without an obedience that comes by way of the cross is to become a rebel. But first, let us see why the Israelites could not enter the promised land.

> So we see that they were not able to enter, because of their unbelief. (Hebrews 3:19)

Like the Israelites of old who were not permitted to enter the promised land, we too cannot claim the promises of

God until we come before the mercy seat full of faith that He does talk to His children. Some might, in presumptuous[2] religious pride, claim a promise as their own, but God will reject such rebels because their faith must come from heaven's faith. A faith that is full of and overflowing with obedience inspired by the Holy Spirit.

> It still remains that some will enter that rest, and those who formerly had the gospel preached to them did not go in, because of their disobedience. (Hebrews 4:6)

Disobedience and Unbelief

We need to note well that Hebrews 3:19 declares they could not enter because of "unbelief," while Hebrews 4:6 declares they could not enter because of "disobedience." Both are true. The man who does not believe God will not obey Him. The man who does not believe God speaks will not listen. And the man who does not listen for God idolizes his Bible study. With this in mind, it is easy to understand why Jesus said that we must obey a God that is "in heaven" if we desire salvation. A man cannot just obey the Bible and expect to go to heaven. That is like using our own tools[3] to build an altar to God, and to become like Saul who went where God sent him but refused to listen for His voice. Saul did his religious duty, he obeyed the Scriptures but didn't listen for God Himself to speak.

> But Samuel replied: "Does the Lord delight in burnt offerings and sacrifices as much as in obeying the voice of the Lord? To obey is better than sacrifice, and to heed is better than the fat of rams." (1 Samuel 15:22)

We must hear from God what His will[4] is for us each day, obeying the Father "who is in heaven."

> Not everyone who says to me, "Lord, Lord," will enter the kingdom of heaven, but only he who does the will of my Father who is in heaven. (Matthew 7:21)

Divine Power

Consider Jesus and the fact we must walk like Him in this world.[5] Jesus heard the Voice of God and we are commanded to listen for this voice and follow the one who speaks to us from heaven. Jesus spent the night in prayer and then chose twelve apostles. The Holy Spirit that God gives us is our Counselor and a very personal Spirit of Truth that will be with us throughout all of eternity.[6] The Holy Spirit is part of the Trinity of God and the living God in us. If we expect God to give us more of His Holy Spirit, then we must come before Him with obedience in mind.

There is a power in God's voice. It can create a universe, it can sustain heaven and breaks trees of cedar.[7] If we seek to obey His voice, grace and mercy will be given us in abundance. Therefore, we are without excuse for not living a perfect life in Jesus. As 2 Peter 1:3 tells us, "His divine power has given us everything we need for life and godliness through our knowledge of him who called us by his own glory and goodness." Only our stubbornness, sinfulness, and hard heartedness keep us from walking just as Jesus did in this world.

You can easily spot a mocker who declares they have the Holy Spirit, because they obviously do not practice what Jesus taught. Though they claim to have the Holy Spirit, they do not obey the living God. In fact, we have known many a preacher and ministry organization that, in terms of doctrine, teach correctly the message of the cross, but do not obey the Holy Spirit. They obey their own set of guidelines and understanding of Scripture, but they do not hear the voice of God that instructs them in how, when, and what to obey. As Jesus said, "You diligently study the Scriptures because you think that by them you possess eternal life. These are the Scriptures that testify about me, yet you refuse to come to me to have life."[8]

In the book of 2 Peter chapter 1, verse 4 we are told that the precious promises of God empower us to overcome sin. But like Joshua in the Old Testament, the taking of the Promised Land, or promises of God for us, requires that we do so at the leading of the Holy Spirit. We must, like Joshua, meet the army of God and follow where the army is commanded to go.[9] It is not for us to pick our battles or how to fight them, it is the Spirit's sword, the living Word of God, that does the fighting.[10]

The Way of the Cross

Obedience does not mean that we go to the Bible, pick a passage and seek to obey that ink on paper. This causes us to become foolish Galatians spell-bound by our own bewitchment. Like a witch that believes she has the words to the incantations correct, those in Christ who do not obey by way of the cross foolishly believe they have correct doctrine. Because they do not hear God concerning doctrine, they believe their doctrine is correct. For, "all a man's ways seem innocent to him."[11] Only the voice of God can give us sound doctrine.[12]

> You foolish Galatians! Who has bewitched you? Before your very eyes Jesus Christ was clearly portrayed as crucified. (Galatians 3:1)

Only by seeing Jesus Christ clearly crucified and understanding what that means can we gain the Promised Land. In short, there is no resurrected life without the crucifixion. Jesus told all who come after Him to be saved, that they must pick up a daily cross.[13] This is the third element that determines whether a man or woman has ears to hear correctly or not. So many people go wrong because they have not allowed the cross to kill them. They have rushed ahead believing that their own voices are the voice of God. Jeremiah spoke boldly against the corruption of his day and his words are needed more now than ever. For the church has rejected the offensive, painful cross of Christ and embraced their opinions about God. As each man claims that his own words are the voice of God, we see more corruption in the church. Each person doing what they want, pleasing their flesh, and doing their will in the name of the Lord. They may quote Scripture, but the "words of the living God" have been distorted.

> But you must not mention "the oracle of the Lord" again, because every man's own word becomes his oracle and so you distort the words of the living God, the Lord Almighty, our God. (Jeremiah 23:36)

If we want ears to hear then we must allow the cross to crucify us so that we can hear clearly. For after crucifixion is the resurrected life with all of its blessings. We must feel terrified of delighting in our religious opinions and wait upon the cross to crucify the fleshly desires that would distort what God wants. For as God warns in Deuteronomy 29:19, "When such a person hears the words of this oath, he invokes a blessing on himself and therefore thinks, 'I will be safe, even though I persist in going my own way.' This will bring disaster on the watered land as well as the dry." We cannot apply God's Word in any way that we choose. Just as Jesus not only let God show Him what to say, but also how to say it, so should we.[14] After all, only a fool delights in airing his own opinion. And our greatest danger as Christians in hearing God is trying to enter the Promised Land by our religious, biblical opinions.[15]

HEARING AIDES

- Why do we need faith, obedience, and crucifixion of self in order to hear God?

- What happens if we obey Scripture or doctrines without faith and belief that we can hear the voice of God?

- Take a moment and ask yourself, "Am I willing to die to self so that I can hear God?"

Chapter 5

Growing Up

Peter, when first hearing the voice of Jesus to come follow Him, fell down and cried, "Go away from me, Lord; I am a sinful man!"[1] But Peter had a lot of growing up to do. In fact, it wasn't until he had been with Jesus for over three years that Peter went out and wept bitterly as a man of faith. The brokenness at the start was child's play compared to what he experienced next to the cross. How foolishly we think we have received all the brokenness there is for us in Jesus. Peter understood all too well that we must grow up if we want to understand what the voice of the Lord tells us.

> Like newborn babies, crave pure spiritual milk, so that by it you may grow up in your salvation. (1 Peter 2:2)

How sad to see many who have just come to Christ, think they can hear and understand the voice of the Lord. Sadder still, so many churches let this assumption be accepted among new converts. Leaders feel so afraid of offending new members, driving them from the church, that they remove the offense that could mature them. Throughout the New Testament, being born again is compared to childbirth.[2] The Bible clearly portrays that, like babies, we must grow up in Jesus Christ.

Learning to Speak

No newborn can understand what his parents say. Even those who have had their parents speak to them in the womb cannot understand words once they are born. It takes years to speak, understand, and gain wisdom from what a parent says to a child. Indeed, many a parent can testify that their children did not really gain wisdom until much later in life. So it is with us in Christ. It is a long hard narrow road to maturity and you must give God time to teach you. We must allow the cross to do its painful work daily if we desire to gain ears that can hear. Paul communicated this to the Corinthians.

> When I was a child, I talked like a child, I thought like a child, I reasoned like a child. When I became a man, I put childish ways behind me. (1 Corinthians 13:11)

Until we allow the cross to crucify us to our childish ways in the Lord, we will not have mature ears that can hear. Let us then in humility let the Lord teach us as little children. Jesus said we must come to Him as little children, and we only hinder our maturity when we think of ourselves too highly. We must think of ourselves with sober judgment, according to the measure of faith God gives us at the time.[3] Even after thirty years of following the voice of the Lord, I still have certain areas where I need the help of others, areas where I know my flesh remains too strong to hear God.

Like a Child

At first, like a baby, everything had to be tested with great effort. I was a baby crawling on the floor, later I toddled across the room and then walked. It took years before I could run and there were a lot of bumps along the way. This is why the Bible tells us to be slow to speak and quick to listen.[4] If a man interrupts me constantly I know he interrupts the Lord when the Holy Spirit tries to talk to him. If a man always listens to me and never says "Amen," then I know he too never acts on what God wants to tell him. If a man continues to say, "I know that," then I know God cannot teach that man anything new. If someone always jumps in with their opinions of why something cannot be done, I know they are defiant in faith and will always tell God something can't be done that He asks of them. How we listen, or don't listen to others, shows us how well we can hear God.

In fact, many individuals never grow unto maturity because they remain too stubborn to humble themselves. Let me repeat it, we must come to Jesus as little children.

> And he said: "I tell you the truth, unless you change and become like little children, you will never enter the kingdom of heaven. Therefore, whoever humbles himself like this child is the greatest in the kingdom of heaven." (Matthew 18:3–4)

When someone is born again they must humble themselves and admit that when it comes to the voice of the Lord they are infants, babies that can't feed, clothe, or even burp themselves. They are helpless, needing constant protection and guidance. As time goes on the child must pass through the toddler state, the teenage stage and finally, years later, adulthood.

Jesus said we must "change" but few are willing to be changed into a child. We want to keep our dignity as sinful adults while we try to be children of God. Such a combination can never mature you into a man or woman of God. In fact, this is a salvation issue. Jesus said that unless we become like little children we cannot go to heaven.

A child must be taught everything. So too, we must allow God to teach us everything. What words mean, how to use those words, and which words are bad words. We must let God tell us what He means just as a parent must explain to a child what they are saying. Any parent can tell you they often have to say to a child, "That is not what I meant."

Gaining ears to hear means that, instead of us telling God what the Bible means, we let God explain it to us. Instead of us telling God what we will do for Him today, we let God tell us what He wants us to do. We must let those who have suffered on the cross, putting their flesh to death, teach us how to hear God's voice. Unfortunately, too much pride fills the church today for men to allow a godly man to teach them how to hear God's voice. The vast majority in the church would cringe at being addressed as mere children in the Lord.

> I have no greater joy than to hear that my children are walking in the truth. (3 John 1:4)

Admitting Our Immaturity

How easily we become indignant when God either personally, or through those more spiritually mature than us, reveal the fact that we are mere babes, children in Christ. If we want to gain ears that can hear, then all pride must be confessed in the Light so that we can be healed. When we make mistakes in what we think we heard, we must admit our sin and look to the reason we failed.

Think of the twelve apostles. For over three years what did Jesus reveal to them about themselves? Every child learns by being corrected and corrected a lot. Jesus constantly rebuked, admonished, and put them in situations that revealed their pride and sinful nature. Jesus even went so far as to refer to Peter as Satan. God desperately wanted to break their self-assuredness and pride. Jesus applied the first pains of the cross that would execute their self-righteous dignity. Even with natural children we speak of the pains of growing up, how much more when we as Christians know we must carry our cross as we head toward heaven? We can only gain ears to hear by humiliation on the cross.

We must admit we need breast milk and baby food. Understand that solid food is for the mature who have constantly heard the voice of God training them to know right from wrong.[5]

HEARING AIDES

- Why is it important to come to Jesus as a child if we hope to mature?

- What areas in your life do you find it difficult to receive instruction from someone else?

- List some things you know that God has been trying to instruct you in. Stop and pray for God to crucify these things so that you can have ears to hear.

Chapter 6

The Need for Self Crucified

> The disciples did not understand any of this. Its meaning was hidden from them, and they did not know what he was talking about. (Luke 18:34)

What kept the disciples from understanding what Jesus told them? Jesus spoke to them about being resurrected from the dead but the meaning of what He said was completely hidden from them. Why could they not understand and why was God not able to give them wisdom? I do not use the term "able" in the sense that God is not powerful enough, but to illustrate clearly that we ourselves stop the power of God from working in our lives. Just as Jesus could not do any miracles in His hometown because of unbelief, so too we cannot comprehend what God tells us because self blocks the way.[1]

Take a loaf of bread for example. The disciples could not understand a miracle that involved loaves of bread because their hearts were hard. Jesus did not ask what school they went to but told them why they were deaf and why they could not remember. They had hard hearts. They could only hear their own voice and remained so self-absorbed all they felt concerned with was themselves.

> Aware of their discussion, Jesus asked them: "Why are you talking about having no bread? Do you still not see or understand? Are your hearts hardened? Do you have eyes but fail to see, and ears but fail to hear? And don't you remember?" (Mark 8:17–18)

Let us not sin by thinking we are any better than the apostles. Self, with all of its pride, will, desires, and wisdom, keeps us from hearing what Jesus says, let alone obeying what He commands us to do. Remember the passage we looked at in Galatians? The one that spoke of Jesus being clearly portrayed as crucified? We must see our flesh crucified on the cross. We must understand, by illumination from the Holy Spirit, our total inability to understand and obey what God speaks to us. Our hearts, minds, and flesh are mixed with so many evil motives that the only solution is to kill it. It must die on the cross as we pick up our daily cross if we want to gain ears that can hear.

Golden Calf

Everything that we think we hear God tell us to do must be tested by the cross of Christ. For in this world, from beginning to end, the matter of hearing God's voice flows from and to the cross. For this reason, Paul wrote in 1 Corinthians 2:2 "I resolved to know nothing while I was with you except Jesus Christ and him crucified." It takes resolve not to give way to our wisdom about godly matters! It takes resolve to say "No" to fleshly desires. It takes resolve to not make a golden calf in the name of the Lord so that we can fool ourselves into thinking we do God's will while we really please our flesh.

> When Aaron saw this, he built an altar in front of the calf and announced, "Tomorrow there will be a festival to the Lord." (Exodus 32:5)

The vast majority in the church today who declare they hear the voice of God tell them to do something, and claim that God gives them wisdom about Scripture, in reality worship a golden calf in the name of the Lord. To them their doctrine, actions, and goals are as shiny as gold, but it is the golden calf that allows them to please themselves in the name of the Lord.

Lose Our Lives

The solution is a cross that causes us to hate our own lives.[2] To hate our time, comfort, wisdom, knowledge, desires, wants, and wills. Until a man hates his life, he is in no position to claim that he has ears to hear. Jesus did not command us to deny only certain aspects of ourselves.

> The man who loves his life will lose it, while the man who hates his life in this world will keep it for eternal life. (John 12:25)

Jesus said we must deny self—all of self. All of who we are. To be born again means that yourself, who you are, is killed and a totally different person is born.[3] Crucifixion is a slow process and God wants to crucify a little bit more of you daily. If you want ears to hear, then your ears must be killed by way of the cross.

A lack of Bible knowledge does not keep us from understanding God. It is not that we don't have the proper steps down that enable us to hear and understand God speaking to us. We cannot hear because our hearts remain hard. God repeats in the book of Mark that the disciples could not understand what Jesus said because they had hard hearts. Many go to Bible college, yet do not understand anything about the power of the cross. Why? Not from lack of Bible study and prayer, but because their hearts remain hardened.

> . . . for they had not understood about the loaves; their hearts were hardened. (Mark 6:52)

Our Opinions

The disciples' fleshly ears had heard Jesus speak words of wisdom and their ears had heard the deaf shout for joy when healed. Yet their ears could not understand anything about Jesus or what He was about. Their notions of Him were vague ideas about Him being the Messiah. Just as it is with most people in the church, the apostles had a simple understanding that Jesus was the Messiah but that was about it. How often we too think we understand the will of God yet are as deaf as the disciples. Only the cross can crucify us so that we gain heavenly ears that can hear and understand what God wills.

Many churches and denominations do not have ears to hear, yet think they hear God. This delusion is most severe among those who think they teach the message of the cross. How easy it is for us to think our godless chatter is godly prayer. How easily we call false knowledge the wisdom that comes from the Holy Spirit.

> Timothy, guard what has been entrusted to your care. Turn away from godless chatter and the opposing ideas of what is falsely called knowledge, which some have professed and in so doing have wandered from the faith. Grace be with you. (1 Timothy 6:20–21)

Many have wandered from the faith. Not necessarily in giant leaps of forsaking the Lord, but in small missteps from the faith. They take one small opinion or desire and call it the voice of the Lord. The best example of this was when Jesus talked to a woman at the well about eternal life, while His disciples tried to find something to eat. Although they traveled with Jesus, following Him everywhere, their bellies came first. The twelve called Him Rabbi, or Teacher, but they had not learned anything.

> Meanwhile his disciples urged him, "Rabbi, eat something." (John 4:31)

Only God's grace can crucify us and rescue us from a hard heart. If we want ears to hear then we must let God break the hard ground of our hearts. Opinions must die, our wills must be opposed and our most sacred of doctrines surrendered to the cross the Holy Spirit gives us to carry if we want ears that can hear.

Hearing Aides

- The apostles spent three years listening to every word Jesus spoke, yet never understood His meaning. Why did the cross open their ears to understanding?

- What golden calves do you see in the church today?

- What other voices do you hear in your life? Do you find it hard to crucify these other voices? What things keep your heart hard? List some ways you could soften your heart and open your ears.

Chapter 7

The Shame of the Cross

We come to hear God clearly by way of the cross. Seeing Jesus clearly crucified allows us to understand that the flesh is worthless and keeps us from hearing God. The cross is also a thing of shame, and if we want to gain ears that hear, we must fully embrace the shame of the cross in our lives. No Christian correctly hears God unless they follow Jesus to the cross. As Hebrews tells us, we must fix our eyes on Jesus and ignore the shame of the cross.

> Let us fix our eyes on Jesus, the author and perfecter of our faith, who for the joy set before him endured the cross, scorning its shame, and sat down at the right hand of the throne of God. (Hebrews 12:2)

When someone was crucified, they were crucified naked. Every flaw, weakness, and embarrassment was revealed for all to see. How does this apply to having ears to hear? The answer is found in another question. How much of

God's correction are you willing to take? The more we accept the shame of the cross, the keener our ears become. Remember, the disciples were rebuked and corrected by Jesus for over three years. Before they could experience the power of Pentecost and the guiding of the Holy Spirit in a powerful way, they first had to follow Jesus closer and closer to the cross.

The Word "No"

So it is with us, wisdom is found by being shamed. What is one of the first words a child learns? Right after the words "da-da" or "ma-ma" a child says the word "No." Learning to talk and to listen begins with the word "No." Even when you ask young children if they want ice cream they will often say "No" when they really mean "Yes." Parents must give a lot of correction before the child can form sentences and understand the correct thing to say and do. In short, they must learn to listen for the word "No" and obey that word if they are to stay safe in life. For this reason, God tells us that grace equals the word "No." In Titus 2:12 we read, grace "teaches us to say 'No' . . ." If we want ears that can hear God then we must first learn to hear and accept the word "No" by the grace of God.

Do you want to hear the thoughts of God? Would you like to have ears that can listen to Him so that you can obtain the heart of God? God promises that He will pour out His heart into you and make you to know His thoughts —if—you will respond to His rebukes. So again, we ask, "How much correction can you take? How deeply are you willing to let the cross weaken, shame, and rebuke you?" As with the twelve apostles, so it must be with us if we want to hear Jesus. We must allow Jesus to give us a cross that corrects, convicts, and humbles us in various ways.

Sometime do a study on when the Holy Spirit led men and women in the Bible. Let's nail this down by looking to the book of Proverbs tells us how to get wisdom and what wisdom sounds like. Also mark all the times Proverbs mentions corrections, rebukes, and acceptance of advice.

> If you had responded to my rebuke, I would have poured out my heart to you and made my thoughts known to you. But since you rejected me when I called and no one gave heed when I stretched out my hand, since you ignored all my advice and would not accept my rebuke. (Proverbs 1:23–25)

Taking Advice

We start to gain ears to hear when we allow God to make us afraid. Few are willing to take advice but everyone in pride loves to give advice. Few people sit and listen to advice. Most of the time we want to tell God and others that we already know and understand what they tell us. When we have that attitude we cannot hear what God says and spurn His rebukes.

> Since they hated knowledge and did not choose to fear the Lord, since they would not accept my advice and spurned my rebuke, they will eat the fruit of their ways and be filled with the fruit of their schemes. (Proverbs 1:29–31)

Shutting our ears to the advice and rebukes that God seeks to overwhelm us with, only leaves us with our schemes. All such schemes, though biblically based, are wicked to the core and will end with bitter fruit. Like Saul before he became Paul, who was perfect in biblical terms and kept the Law,[1] but tried to make others[2] blaspheme

God. Undoubtedly Paul said his prayers and felt God blessed his efforts. Yet, he was a violent man that hunted down the disciples of Jesus.[3] It wasn't until Jesus appeared and opposed him on the Damascus road that his ears opened to hear the voice of God. Like Saul, many kick against the goads[4] and refuse to listen to the rebukes, advice, and correction the Lord speaks to us. In fact, many preachers oppose Jesus Christ because they have not let the painful cross rebuke and scold them unto a resurrected life.

Hearing Through Suffering

In the church today we seem to believe that a person can come to God and begin to hear, understand, and obey the Lord all at once. This is like a parent believing that a new born can carry on a conversation moments after birth. It takes years for any Christian to say he or she can hear God correctly. The Lord charges all preachers and teachers to teach His children to have ears to hear.[5] But only teachers who have suffered against sin, allowing the Holy Spirit to repeatedly rebuke, humble, and correct until death to self occurs, can teach God's sheep. After all, the blind cannot lead the blind and the deaf cannot teach others how to hear with their ears. Teachers, preachers, and children of God who cannot tell you of how they suffered on the cross with their sins cannot teach you how to have ears to hear.

> Therefore, since Christ suffered in his body, arm yourselves also with the same attitude, because he who has suffered in his body is done with sin. As a result, he does not live the rest of his earthly life for evil human desires, but rather for the will of God. (1 Peter 4:1–2)

Jesus suffered on the cross and if you want to have ears to hear you too will feel, in a very real physical way, the cross killing your flesh. You will be rebuked by God to the point it hurts and you will feel tempted to scream, "Enough!" Few willingly accept and endure the work of the cross that comes against them. Wave upon wave of advice and rebukes awaits anyone who desires ears that can hear.[6] Want ears that can hear? Desire the thoughts of God? Then answer this question, "How much rebuke will you endure and how much of the shame of the cross are you willing to accept?"

Hearing Aides

- 1 Corinthians 1:28 tells us that "He chose the lowly things of this world and the despised things—and the things that are not—to nullify the things that are—so that no one may boast before him." Why do you think God uses shameful things to teach us wisdom?

- How has God specifically taught you lessons through embarrassing means?

- Why does it take time to learn how to hear God?

- What aspects of the Cross do you find shameful?

- In what areas of your life do you feel you need more of the shame of the cross? Ask yourself, "Am I willing to endure the cross?"

Chapter 8

Teenage Years

If anyone thinks he is something when he is nothing, he deceives himself. (Galatians 6:3)

An eye-catching bumper sticker says, "Hire a teenager while they still know it all." This really describes this stage in life. Teenagers think they are something and that they know everything. In the same way, Christian "teenagers," believers who have been at it for a little while, gain a little experience, a little Bible knowledge and deceive themselves. Many never outgrow this stage and many preachers and Bible college professors are nothing more than overgrown teenagers in the name of Jesus.

Teenagers are still nothing in terms of the world, but they think they are ready to take on the world. The teenage years are the most dangerous time for us as we grow up. In most cases those years set the stage for the rest of our lives. Unless God can win us with His grace our sins are set into our personalities and our course for eternity is laid. At age thirteen the natural rebellion in mankind begins to seek independence. Young children that at one time listened to their parents refuse to do so any longer. What marks a teenager? They think they are wiser and smarter than they really are. This happened to the twelve apostles.

These men followed Jesus for quite some time. They preached, worked, and listened to Jesus. They started out falling at his feet in humility, but soon began to give Jesus advice and suggested ways He should do things. For example, they did not have the faith to cast out demons yet suggested they call fire down from heaven. Did they ask Jesus to call down the fire? No, they asked if "they" could call down fire. Like any teenager, the apostles thought they had power and wisdom.

> When the disciples James and John saw this, they asked, "Lord, do you want us to call fire down from heaven to destroy them?" But Jesus turned and rebuked them. (Luke 9:54–55)

Rebellious Teenagers

Like any wounded teenager when someone upsets them, they vent their full wrath. Many in the church never outgrow this self-assuredness and pride and refuse to let the cross do its maturing work. They remain smart, wise, and full of biblical wisdom so when Jesus seeks to rebuke and correct, they become indignant and shut their ears to the voice of God. Or when God seeks to communicate what His will is for the hour or day, their wisdom and advice silence Him. We know from experience that when a teenager becomes overbearing there is only one of two reactions parents can take, either rebuke and lay down the law or just turn silent. In the same way, God often resorts to the Law but more often just becomes silent until we are ready to listen. It is a dreadful matter when God stops talking to us because of our stubbornness. For all we are left with is our spiritual voice that mocks the things of God. If teenagers are well known for anything, it is refusing advice and not listening. How many in the church are also known for this?

> But they refused to pay attention; stubbornly they turned their backs and stopped up their ears. (Zechariah 7:11)

If you want to grow past this stage then you must once again learn from your mistakes. Again, the more correction you are willing to take, the quicker you will gain ears that can hear God. The more you let the humility of Christ live in you, the quicker you will gain ears to hear.

It is one of the hardest things to admit our mistakes and sins, because pride blinds us to who we really are. Impurity marks this time. Like a teenager, we have some life skills, some logic, and some knowledge, but there is still much of self that must be put to death. Unfortunately when God points out the impurity in our lives, we can only see the noble reasons and excuses. Of course this is an impossible situation. Impurity can never exist with purity and purity can never tolerate impurity. One will overcome the other. Therefore God will often press in harder with the cross during this teenage time and the temptation to rebel and leave will be great. At this stage the Christian seeks to do God's will but also attempts at the same time to do it their way or to get something out of the situation. Since no "impure" person will go to heaven we must fully confess our wisdom and desires as sin when attempting to obey the voice of God.

Misinterpreting God's Voice

During this time in our walk we tend to learn to hear God from the times we misinterpret His voice. Early in our marriage we were houseparents for a group home of mentally disabled men. We saw many of them give their hearts to God and tremendous changes occurred in their lives. Soon, however, Church and State issues arose. This led us to believe that God wanted us to open up our own Christian based group home. After many blunders and even losing money on downpayments on facilities, we realized that we didn't know what God's will was after all. Our pure and noble reasons had to be exposed for what they were—frustration over the situation in the group home circuits. We wanted those people to know Christ, but in our own way and timing, not God's.

> For of this you can be sure: No immoral, impure or greedy person—such a man is an idolater—has any inheritance in the kingdom of Christ and of God. Let no one deceive you with empty words, for because of such things God's wrath comes on those who are disobedient. Therefore do not be partners with them. (Ephesians 5:5–7)

As stated before, impurity cannot co-exist with purity. Therefore, Paul stated we are not to be "partners with" the impure.

Test Everything

When it comes to having ears to hear God, testing correctly the messages we have is paramount to purity. Paul laid down the rule in 1 Thessalonians 5:21 to "test everything." Yes, it takes a lot of work to test everything all day long. Indeed, it requires a lot of effort to work out our salvation with fear and trembling,[1] but it's worth it to hear the voice of God. How do we test everything? By way of the cross.

With guidance and power from the Holy Spirit begin to ask yourself, "Where is my flesh in all of this?" Or say it another way, "Where is the cross of Christ in this?" Just as Jesus always carried His cross and headed toward the cross, so we too, when it comes to hearing and obeying God, know that He always heads us toward Calvary. Any voice that takes us away from the cross is either our voice or the voice of the world and Satan. The Spirit will always want the opposite of what you want.[2] God will never give you what you want until you have been crucified and no longer live.[3] Yes, He will fulfill the "desires of your heart,"[4] but only after your desires match His holiness. There will always be groaning and a battle while you walk this earth.[5] The voice of God will always direct you in ways you do not want to go. If you attend a church or employ a pastor where this conflict is not present you follow a lie.

Many times we may have heard God clearly but still have a lot of self to deny and crucify. I might, for example, hear from God to go do something today, but my flesh sneaks into the situation and I want to do it my way or for some personal enjoyment. Like Judas, whom Jesus put in charge of the money bag but from time to time helped himself to the money,[6] we take from the Lord. In order to mature past the teenage years, we must prepare ourselves for a baptism of fire that will purify us of stubbornness and selfishness. Unless you are willing to rejoice in this you will never gain ears to hear.

> I baptize you with water for repentance. But after me will come one who is more powerful than I, whose sandals I am not fit to carry. He will baptize you with the Holy Spirit and with fire. (Matthew 3:11)

Hearing Aides

- List some behaviors common to teens. Compare these traits to your spiritual walk with God.

- What impure motives lie in your heart? Take them before God and ask Him to purify them.

- In what ways can you test everything, especially your motives?

Chapter 9

God's Paths, Commands, Precepts, Ways, and Laws

> Oh, the depth of the riches of the wisdom and knowledge of God! How unsearchable his judgments, and his paths beyond tracing out! (Romans 11:33)

If God's paths are unsearchable, why do we foolishly think we can understand and apply Scripture? The ways of God are just not simple. One time the Spirit of the Lord may have you offend someone, then the next time commend the same person. He may have you hide, then go out in the open rebuke, or be gentle.[1] Simply put, we cannot predict the mind of the Lord. A Spirit-filled Christian is called to follow the wind—an impossible thing to do. Indeed, Jesus said that those led of the Spirit, born of the Spirit, are like the wind.[2]

Only a fool thinks he can hear the voice of the Lord after reading the Bible or simply asking Jesus into his heart. Only a fool thinks he can understand the voice of the Lord after graduating from Bible college. The ways of God are unsearchable and we must learn to listen for God's voice before we take each new step. In Proverbs 16:9 it declares, "In his heart a man plans his course, but the Lord determines his steps." Walking with God means we plan a course of righteousness, but we listen for His voice to direct our steps. Those who do not listen for God's voice, allowing the cross to direct their steps, become classic Pharisees. Religious zealots, but having no relationship with God. They are dead in their sins.

We must allow the Holy Spirit to search our hearts and purify our motives. We must allow the cross to crucify and deny self with great fear and trembling if we want to leave our simple ways behind and truly hear the voice of the Lord. Many rejoice in mocking the Word of God, but few actually hear the voice of the living God. Most are happy to mock the voice of God and go about their merry little Christian life.

> How long will you simple ones love your simple ways? How long will mockers delight in mockery and fools hate knowledge? (Proverbs 1:22)

The School of the Lord

Someone entering first grade is not prepared to go to work the next day. Anyone seeking to become a doctor cannot, after a week of medical school, open an office to heal the sick. In fact, it takes years before a medical student ever seeks patients. In the same way, if we want to have ears to hear we must first enter the school of the Lord and be taught by God.

> It is written in the Prophets: "They will all be taught by God." Everyone who listens to the Father and learns from him comes to me. (John 6:45)

Sadly, churches and ministries seldom teach new believers that they must enter the school of the Lord. Oh, we cart them off to Bible college and put them through a Bible study programs. But the way of the cross, where God teaches each man or woman, is seldom understood and even less lived. School is not for action, but for learning. It is a time of quietness, tests, and listening to the teacher. The more noisy the classroom the less the class can hear the teacher and learn the material presented. Few people like school because it's a laborious process where slowly but surely one gains knowledge. Often a student will ask, "How will this fact help me? How does this apply in the real world?" Later, if the student learns the lessons well, he comes to understand the importance of studying facts that didn't seem to apply to daily life. So it is with us who want to hear God's voice. We must store the Word in our hearts. We must store things about God's Word we do not understand at the time, but will greatly matter to our salvation later on down the road. We hide the Word, and God teaches us from what we have hidden in our hearts.

> I have hidden your word in my heart that I might not sin against you. Praise be to you, O Lord; teach me your decrees. (Psalm 119:11–12)

Quiet Before God

We have much to learn. There is not just the law of God, but also the ways, paths, truths, and wisdom of God. All with distinct characteristics and power of their own. We must hide in our hearts this Word in all of its varied forms. A young Christian should sit alone[3] quietly putting the Word in his heart like seeds planted in the soil. Not reading and storing the Word with commentary, opinion, and ideas, but letting the seed fall into soft soil. Being content to let God be God.[4] Letting God provide the definitions and applications to His Word. The Word will produce the plant it desires and there is no need for you to apply your thoughts and efforts to try and make it grow. Not only will it damage the plant, but there is the very real danger you will kill the plant. God will send the rain and the snow upon the seed of His Word. He will ensure that it accomplishes what He wills and wants, if the soil of your heart is soft.[5]

> As the rain and the snow come down from heaven, and do not return to it without watering the earth and making it bud and flourish, so that it yields seed for the sower and bread for the eater, so is my word that goes out from my mouth: It will not return to me empty, but will accomplish what I desire and achieve the purpose for which I sent it. (Isaiah 55:10–11)

In short, let God teach you what His Word, truths, paths, and commands mean for you personally. Let God apply the Word in your life and let Him crucify your church's doctrine and way of doing things so that you can gain ears that hear.

The Starting Point

The first place to start learning to hear the voice of the Holy Spirit is through the Bible. I do not mean that you read the Bible and listen to your own voice, but that as you read the Scripture you let the Holy Spirit teach you what the Word says and means. Let me remind the reader that this can only be done in truth if the offensive and painful cross of Christ is alive and working its death to self.

> As for you, the anointing you received from him remains in you, and you do not need anyone to teach you. But as his anointing teaches you about all things and as that anointing is real, not counterfeit—just as it has taught you, remain in him. (1 John 2:27)

Let the anointing of God teach you what the Bible means and how it should be applied in your life. And when God does not give illumination on a Scripture, remain content and wait for the Lord to reveal the truth to you at the proper time.[6] There are many Scriptures I do not understand even after over twenty years of being a disciple of Jesus. There are certain things that for me the Holy Spirit will not let me explore. So I rest, like a weaned child at a mother's breast, unconcerned about feeding my flesh or having to understand everything.[7] I store them in my heart so that at the proper time God may teach me what it means and show me how His Word should be lived. This is worshipping in spirit and truth.[8] The difference between a Pharisee and a true child of God is that the child of God has been taught directly by the voice of the Lord.

> I have not departed from your laws, for you yourself have taught me. (Psalm 119:102)

The Psalmist did not disobey the Bible because he was willing to be taught directly and personally by God. Until a man can say that the Lord Himself has taught him, he cannot say he is a disciple of Jesus. But to be taught by God means that a man is often rebuked and corrected by God Himself. While that correction may come through a man, the true disciple will sense the voice of the Lord in it. The Word of God made alive by the Holy Spirit becomes a lamp that shines on our faults, sins, and failures. And when we hear that voice we have a choice to either ignore those sins or to heed the correction that leads to life. How sad, but most people love the whitewash[9] that churches offer and few allow the cross to expose and crucify their sins.

> For these commands are a lamp, this teaching is a light, and the corrections of discipline are the way to life. (Proverbs 6:23)

If you desire ears that can hear then you must let God show you His paths, His truth, His laws, and His commands by way of the cross and His Holy Spirit. You must let God personally teach you, and as a result God will be your Savior and your hope "all day long." Without this, you will never gain ears that can hear.

> Show me your ways, O Lord, teach me your paths; guide me in your truth and teach me, for you are God my Savior, and my hope is in you all day long. (Psalm 25:4–5)

God must guide us in unsearchable ways so we only have need to, as Peter writes, "prepare your minds for action."[10] Set our minds on things above[11] and ears to hear will be given us.

Hearing Aides

- Why is it foolish to think we understand God's ways by simply reading the Bible?

- What keeps a man from departing from the Scriptures?

- Why is it important to hear from the Holy Spirit when interpreting Scripture?

- What Scriptures would you like to understand more fully?

- Take some time to examine your heart to see what keeps you from enlightenment. Ask the Holy Spirit to crucify your own opinions in these areas.

Chapter 10

Dreams, Visions, and Spiritual Gifts

Follow the way of love and eagerly desire spiritual gifts, especially the gift of prophecy. (1 Corinthians 14:1)

Spiritual gifts are just as much for today as they were when the apostles started the first church. Why else would Paul urge us to eagerly desire them? A person filled with a love and faith that comes from heaven will eagerly desire spiritual gifts for the sake of others. Those weighed down with pride will not believe they exist today. We do not have time to discuss how spiritual gifts must be used properly or to defend the fact they occur today. Rather we want to discover their place in hearing God.

Children are fascinated by magical things and so it is with spiritual gifts, dreams, and visions. Immature children in the Lord remain enchanted by the gifts and seldom use them for their intended purpose. In discussing the gift of tongues for example, Paul declares that unbelievers, and those who do not understand, are fascinated by the gift of tongues. Those more mature could care less that a word from the Lord was spoken in a tongue. Rather, they want to know what the tongue means and how to apply it in obedience to the Lord.

> Tongues, then, are a sign, not for believers but for unbelievers; prophecy, however, is for believers, not for unbelievers. (1 Corinthians 14:22)

Obedience That Flows

The prophecy, that is, the understanding of a message in tongues is for believers. The tongue, or different language, is for the unbeliever. Where you see a group emphasizing that a sign of the Holy Spirit is evident in speaking in tongues, you find mere babes in Christ. God does indeed speak through tongues, dreams, and visions, but it is the obedience that flows from such manifestations that matters. Therefore Paul, when discussing the vision of the Lord on the Damascus road, emphasized not the vision but the obedience that followed.

> So then, King Agrippa, I was not disobedient to the vision from heaven. First to those in Damascus, then to those in Jerusalem and in all Judea, and to the Gentiles also, I preached that they should repent and turn to God and prove their repentance by their deeds. That is why the Jews seized me in the temple courts and tried to kill me. (Acts 26:19–21)

Paul declared clearly that he was "not disobedient to the vision from heaven." And the Jews didn't seek to kill Paul because he had a vision, but because he sought to obey that vision. Remember, God only gives the Holy Spirit to those who obey Him.[1] So ask yourself a very important question. Why should God give you more dreams, visions, or speak to your heart if you do not obey what He has already spoken? To approach miraculous matters of God we need to look no further than Psalm 119.

> Let me understand the teaching of your precepts; then I will meditate on your wonders. (Psalm 119:27)

Using Gifts Wisely

Let us not behave like immature children, ignorant and enthralled with the box the gift came in. Rather, let us use the gifts, dreams, and visions God gives us with reverence and awe. Pray and plead, first and foremost, that God would teach you His precepts. And after you have gained some understanding by way of the cross, you then will meditate on His wonders. After all, God gives us the miraculous, not to entertain us, but to increase the righteous obedience of His beloved children, just as any father delights in the happy obedience of his children.

Think of how Paul was told by God, as recorded in Acts 27, that the ship he traveled on would have to sink with everything destroyed. In fact, in order for everyone to be saved, they would have to let go of their lifeboat. How seldom we are willing to let our lifeboat go, to give up all, as Paul did. No wonder God cannot speak to us and no wonder we are not a blessing to others. Instead, like babies, we remain enthralled with spiritual gifts and miss the whole point of what God speaks.

Without a firm understanding and obedience to the precepts of God, dreams, visions, and gifts only support the sinful flesh of man. We often see this on "Christian" TV and in many churches. For one thing, dreams can often occur because we feel burdened and are not at rest in the Lord.[2] In short, we sleep in sin and dream dreams that we assume are

God giving us answers. More likely we dream our sinful schemes to fix a problem or achieve something we want.

We should walk with the utmost gentleness when it comes to these aspects of God's voice. It is easy to misunderstand God's intentions when He speaks clearly, how much more when God speaks through dreams and visions. This is why Paul wrote that we should weigh everything carefully.

> Two or three prophets should speak, and the others should weigh carefully what is said. (1 Corinthians 14:29)

In fact, scripturally no one is allowed to speak in tongues in public unless someone can interpret the tongue. It is far too easy to hear what we want to hear rather than what God actually wants to tell us. It is also too easy to say what we want God to say, rather than let Him speak His will.[3]

Our Full Attention

God made our ears to pick up noise more clearly in front of us, because we should always seek the face of God and listen to Him. We need to give Him our full and undivided attention. There is nothing worse than a child who will not pay attention to advice or accept love when it's offered. Ours hearts should burn to seek the face of God, which means we stand face to face with Him who speaks to us.[4] If dreams do not lead us to seek the face of God, we miss the whole point for the reason He sends marvelous gifts. After all, dreams, visions, and miracles are small matters compared to what they really mean and point us to.

> "Let the prophet who has a dream tell his dream, but let the one who has my word speak it faithfully. For what has straw to do with grain?" declares the Lord. (Jeremiah 23:28)

Straw has its uses, but the grain the straw supported provides bread and food to man and animals. With any miraculous working of God if we want ears to hear, we must seek the grain and deemphasize the miracle that brought forth the grain. Let us have hearts that are never satisfied until we talk with and listen to God as a lover loves their beloved. Let us be a people that feel burdened by sin and long for God to fully remove the curse of it. Let us seek God not because we get things from Him, see visions, or have dreams, but because we want to see His face and hear His voice.[5] "I will go out and be a lying spirit in the mouth of all his prophets."[6] Let us be sure we are seeking holiness about spiritual gifts or God might send a lying spirit to work poetic justice in our lives.

On the other hand, let us not demean the miracles of God and despise prophecies because they may be His voice encouraging us about the future for our lives.[7] Then we will have a heart that provides us with ears to hear.

Hearing Aides

- Why would we need spiritual gifts today?

- Why do you think that men often overemphasize or deemphasize the gifts?

- In what ways have you misinterpreted or ignored miraculous gifts?

- Does your heart long for more of God? Ask God to work dreams and visions in your life, but plead with Him to use them for His glory.

Chapter 11

God's Voice and Unity

> My brothers, some from Chloe's household have informed me that there are quarrels among you. What I mean is this: One of you says, "I follow Paul"; another, "I follow Apollos"; another, "I follow Cephas"; still another, "I follow Christ." Is Christ divided? Was Paul crucified for you? Were you baptized into the name of Paul? (1 Corinthians 1:11–13)

People who make excuses about coming to church, or who refuse to obey Scripture, often exclaim, "But there are so many churches with other ideas." Indeed, there are many different churches, denominations, and opinions about God. However, Paul still asks, "Is Christ divided?"

The Christian community has not only become accustomed to, but now considers division as a good thing. Dare we say, it seems to the church today that to hold various opinions is a holy thing. For example, most would consider you a foolish reader if you said, "I agree with everything in this book." You might be accused of being a brainwashed zombie that can't think for yourself. This attitude underscores why the first church was considered a cult. For, not only were they one in heart, but also in mind.

> All the believers were one in heart and mind. (Acts 4:32a)

True Unity

Such unity occurred because they could hear the Holy Spirit teach them the true meaning of God's Word. Think again of children in first grade. Everyone must agree that one plus one equals two. No good teacher would allow each person in the class to decide for themselves what one plus one equals. Each pupil must accept the fact that one plus one equals two or they will fail. If we are disciples of Jesus, taught by the Holy Spirit, then unity will not occur on just a few basic things, but even on the deep things of God. For this reason Paul could make the following appeal.

> I appeal to you, brothers, in the name of our Lord Jesus Christ, that all of you agree with one another so that there may be no divisions among you and that you may be perfectly united in mind and thought. (1 Corinthians 1:10)

Not only did he call for unity in mind, but also in thought. In other words, united in the way their minds came to a conclusion. Think of it. Not just united in mind agreeing with doctrines, but in thought, the manner in which someone concludes an issue in their mind.

This is the power of the cross and why David sings in the Psalms that where you find the true unity of God, there you find life forevermore.[1] Unity in the first church was nothing like what we call unity. Today, the word unity has the most generic meaning and implies some airy type of agreement. It certainly does not represent and show the world the steadfast rock, Jesus Christ. And most certainly the world does not see one heart beating in unity with all the hearts in the church. How unlike the first church we are that had one heart and one mind.

We fail at this because we have rejected the cross that crucifies our hearts and thoughts. For all our talk of the cross, we have rejected its power, proven by the bad fruit of division we see today. It is rare, if not impossible, to find two brothers in the Lord perfectly united in heart and mind in Christ, let alone a whole church!

Unity in Jesus Christ is achieved only by hearing the voice of God. As we have seen, it takes time to mature into men and women who can understand deeply the things of God. For this reason Paul taught that if we differ on something in Jesus Christ, God, I repeat God, will make it clear and settle the difference.

> All of us who are mature should take such a view of things. And if on some point you think differently, that too God will make clear to you. (Philippians 3:15)

Crucified Minds

Only those mature in the way of the cross have ears that can hear unto perfect unity. Until you mature in the cross, don't claim the above promise. How sad, with all the effort, debate, resolutions, and creeds bantered about by today's church, we miss the power right before us to come into perfect unity. If we would lay aside all of those things and let the cross crucify our minds and hearts God would give us the heart and mind of Christ. And Christ is not divided, therefore perfect unity would follow.

Let me give the reader an example. Let us say that a brother and I differ on when the Rapture will take place. Whether it is pre, mid, or post tribulation. If we both go into the prayer closet, mature in the power of the cross, and surrender all our thoughts on the issue, God will give us the thoughts of Jesus. Indeed, we would both come out of the prayer closet understanding what Scripture has to say about the end times. Without this unity, we leave the church unprepared and deluded about Christ's return.

We will read the Bible just like we read any other novel or book unless we do one other thing. We must go to Jesus, to the Holy Spirit, and let God give life to the Scriptures we read. The Pharisees, and most Christians today, make the same mistake of reading the Bible and think, because their doctrine seems correct to them, they possess eternal life. But we obtain sound doctrine and unity only by listening to the voice of the Holy Spirit.

> You diligently study the Scriptures because you think that by them you possess eternal life. These are the Scriptures that testify about me, yet you refuse to come to me to have life. (John 5:39–40)

I know many who "diligently study the Scriptures" yet hold no unity, no mind of Christ. They will object to my call for unity by saying, "Then we all have to agree with you," leaving in a huff.

Spiritual Truths

Only God knows what His Word means and what He desires to say through it. All men must give up their voices about the meaning of Scripture and let the Holy Spirit explain its words. Indeed, more than that, we must come to Jesus so that He can show us how the Scriptures apply to our lives. God makes Scripture alive and our voices only make them dead, lifeless ink on paper. As Paul wrote to the Corinthians, your eyes cannot possibly begin to understand what God has in mind. Nor can your ears understand what is spoken in a sermon and how it applies to your life, if the Holy Spirit doesn't speak directly to you. As the following verse shows us, no one "knows the thoughts of God except the Spirit of God." No one! It doesn't matter if a man has gone to Bible college or passed through your church's discipleship program, only God knows His thoughts. And God only speaks His thoughts to those who have ears to hear. It doesn't matter at all if you have brought thousands to the Lord, or your church has grown in numbers, you do not have the thoughts of God on the matter of your church growth unless you have heard His voice by way of the cross.

> However, as it is written: "No eye has seen, no ear has heard, no mind has conceived what God has prepared for those who love him"—but God has revealed it to us by his Spirit. The Spirit searches all things, even the deep things of God. For who among men knows the thoughts of a man except the man's spirit within him? In the same way no one knows the thoughts of God except the Spirit of God. We have not received the spirit of the world but the Spirit who is from God, that we may understand what God has freely given us. This is what we speak, not in words taught us by human wisdom but in words taught by the Spirit, expressing spiritual truths in spiritual words. The man without the Spirit does not accept the things that come from the Spirit of God, for they are foolishness to him, and he cannot understand them, because they are spiritually discerned. (1 Corinthians 2:9–14)

Paul did not preach by the power of man or by applying "human wisdom" to Scripture. Paul had been "taught by the Spirit" and so expressed "spiritual truths in spiritual words." Most preaching and counsel today is nothing more than men stealing words taught by other men.[2] The spirit of the world says a man must go to a university and read books to gain an education; to take the mind God has given him and to apply it to a school of learning. How many approach Bible study from the spirit of the world? How many Bible colleges teach with the same spirit of the world where the reliance is not on the Holy Spirit and the cross, but what they think the Greek and Hebrew mean? This only underscores the foolishness of man. To be impressed that someone can tell you what the Greek or Hebrew means, shows you know nothing about the power of the Holy Spirit. After all, what is the definition of the Greek and Hebrew, but just another interpretation into a language, and every Bible translation claims to reflect the original language. After all, what did the Greeks do? They couldn't turn to their Bible teacher and ask, "What does the Greek say?" Listening to the voice of the Holy Spirit may seem like foolishness to many, but this only shows how true God is to His Word. Without hearing the voice of the Holy Spirit no man will accept the Bible's true meaning.

> The man without the Spirit does not accept the things that come from the Spirit of God, for they are foolishness to him, and he cannot understand them, because they are spiritually discerned. (1 Corinthians 2:14)

Unity by the Spirit

When Paul and Peter had a disagreement it was the cross that solved the problem. Peter didn't become all defensive and say to Paul, "Hey, I have been in the Lord longer than you. I walked with Jesus, you only saw him on the road to Damascus." Pride had been crucified in Peter enough that he repented immediately and unity was restored.[3] And when Paul had a disagreement with Barnabas, the cross revealed to all which man had the grace of God on their side. The unity of the Spirit was maintained until Barnabas learned his lessons.

> They had such a sharp disagreement that they parted company. Barnabas took Mark and sailed for Cyprus, but Paul chose Silas and left, commended by the brothers to the grace of the Lord. (Acts 15:39–40)

If you think this perfect unity is not possible you will never receive ears that can hear. After all, why should God talk to the doubtful and the unbelieving? If we cannot pray as Paul did for a spirit of unity as we follow Jesus then you might as well become a Buddhist.

> May the God who gives endurance and encouragement give you a spirit of unity among yourselves as you follow Christ Jesus. (Romans 15:5)

This kind of unity, that comes from the love of heaven into a church, is difficult to obtain. No doubt about it, our flesh does not want to give up its thoughts and ways. We each want to be something in the church. We want to think we are correct on certain points and are unwilling to give up the way we come to our conclusions. But if we, as Ephesians tells us, "make every effort" to listen to the Holy Spirit we will be given "unity" by the Holy Spirit.

> Make every effort to keep the unity of the Spirit through the bond of peace. There is one body and one Spirit—just as you were called to one hope when you were called—one Lord, one faith, one baptism; one God and Father of all, who is over all and through all and in all. (Ephesians 4:3–6)

Every effort to surrender our lives, pick up a cross, and allow the Holy Spirit to rob us of our thoughts, will produce a unity where everyone with a full heart declares "one Lord, one faith, one baptism." Anything less than this slaps Christ in the face. Anything else called unity is a lie. And all who allow the Lord to give them ears to hear will discover the joy of God granting life forever more upon brothers who live in unity.

Hearing Aides

- What is missing in most Bible studies today? What has been missing in your own study of the Scriptures?

- How can we be united in heart and mind?

- What things in your life keep you from having the mind of Christ?

Chapter 12

How to Hear God Through Others

> . . . not to mention that you owe me your very self. (Philemon 1:19b)

In our pride, we hate to think that we owe someone for our very self. For anyone to suggest that he is a father to us in the Lord and we should respect and listen to him, grates against our flesh.

> Even though you have ten thousand guardians in Christ, you do not have many fathers, for in Christ Jesus I became your father through the gospel. Therefore I urge you to imitate me. (1 Corinthians 4:15–16)

"I don't want to follow another man," is the usual justification for rejecting godly advice. "I don't want to be taken in by another," is the normal excuse for rejecting a fact that someone may be more mature than us in the Lord. Our independent, prideful, and self-satisfied Christianity has produced a hotbed of fertile ground for rebelling against

God. While on the surface of things these are valid concerns, but upon digging deeper we discover it is a cover up for sin. This is easy to see because God has promised to protect us from every false Christian and church, if we only die to ourselves. In Proverbs, God promises that He holds our victory and will shield—protect and guard us from the ways of wicked man, if, I repeat *if*, our walk is blameless. Not in the sense that we are perfect, but blameless in keeping a good conscience that confesses sin the moment God shows us. If we repent deeply as He leads, then we shall become blameless in His sight by the blood of Jesus.[1]

> For the Lord gives wisdom, and from his mouth come knowledge and understanding. He holds victory in store for the upright, he is a shield to those whose walk is blameless, for he guards the course of the just and protects the way of his faithful ones. Then you will understand what is right and just and fair—every good path. For wisdom will enter your heart, and knowledge will be pleasant to your soul. Discretion will protect you, and understanding will guard you. Wisdom will save you from the ways of wicked men, from men whose words are perverse, who leave the straight paths to walk in dark ways. (Proverbs 2:6–13)

God's Protection

If we have ears to hear, the very mouth of God gives us knowledge and understanding and protects us from false brothers. I do not have to walk around all paranoid about being taken in by another man, because God has promised to deliver from every false doctrine. All I need to do is listen for His voice and guidance. Just as God delivered Paul, so too, will He protect us if we die to ourselves.[2] The mere fact we know the Father's voice means that we can run from unfamiliar voices and God protects us long before any real danger occurs.[3]

Whenever I have almost slipped into being taken in by someone, I don't blame that person, I blame myself. I ask the Holy Spirit to search my heart and life to reveal what about my flesh was taken in by a man. God is always faithful to speak and show why I was taken in and I can then submit it to God to be crucified unto death. If Adam had done this in the Garden of Eden, his flesh would not have desired to eat the forbidden fruit.

Speaking Through Men

Proverbs 15:22 tells us that, "Plans fail for lack of counsel, but with many advisers they succeed." But how do we know which counselors to listen to? How can we tell when God speaks through a man or not? The greatest danger is that we might accept advice if we think someone is godly. If we believe someone to be a trusted brother or sister and godly in our own sight, then we will accept their advice; especially if it agrees with what we want to hear. Scripture reveals that we should pay no attention to any man but to listen for the voice of God; the presence of the Lord working through that man. Maybe even listen to a donkey, as was the case with Balaam.

The main point here is, most people are just too prideful to accept God speaking through anyone. In our pride we must have the voice of God come in certain ways, and by all means it has to say what we think it should say. Like Naaman we go away angry and full of rage if God doesn't come to us how we expect or in the tone we like.

> Elisha sent a messenger to say to him, "Go, wash yourself seven times in the Jordan, and your flesh will be restored and you will be cleansed." But Naaman went

> away angry and said, "I thought that he would surely come out to me and stand and call on the name of the Lord his God, wave his hand over the spot and cure me of my leprosy. Are not Abana and Pharpar, the rivers of Damascus, better than any of the waters of Israel? Couldn't I wash in them and be cleansed?" So he turned and went off in a rage. Naaman's servants went to him and said, "My father, if the prophet had told you to do some great thing, would you not have done it? How much more, then, when he tells you, 'Wash and be cleansed'!" (2 Kings 5:10–13)

Know this, when God speaks He will always, I repeat *always*, seek to humble you. But like Naaman we want to be told "to do some great thing" before we will act. We want people to make a fuss over us because we think ourselves worthy. We want men to "come out to" us and "stand and call on the name of the Lord," to "wave his hand over the spot" of our sin and cure us. We want the attention we think we deserve.

Over the years we have known many who cannot accept advice from a woman or from a man, they simply will not listen. My sermons usually have a tone about them that most individuals don't like. My words are not smooth and gentle, and do not allow listeners to keep their pride intact. Therefore people become indignant and thus cannot hear the voice of the Lord speaking through my sermons. So how can we know if God speaks through a man, without following a man? Easy, ask yourself this question at all times. Regardless of who the man is or is not in our eyes, is God speaking through him? Many times I sense God speaking through many different individuals and situations. While great care and testing of everything occurs and a lot of things rejected, the attitude is always one of listening.

Willing to Hear Everything

David always listened and we know he had a heart after God's. King David rode in from a battle with his army and a man began to pelt him with stones. One man against a whole army, yet David could hear the voice of God. David, who in an instant could have defended himself, struck back or allowed someone else to defend him, allows God to talk to him. David with his special guard on his right and left must have felt tempted to strike at God's voice. But David came to the conclusion that the Lord had told the man to throw stones and curse him. Unless you are willing to hear everything from anyone that God would speak to you, don't bother trying to listen.

> As King David approached Bahurim, a man from the same clan as Saul's family came out from there. His name was Shimei son of Gera, and he cursed as he came out. He pelted David and all the king's officials with stones, though all the troops and the special guard were on David's right and left. As he cursed, Shimei said, "Get out, get out, you man of blood, you scoundrel! The Lord has repaid you for all the blood you shed in the household of Saul, in whose place you have reigned. The Lord has handed the kingdom over to your son Absalom. You have come to ruin because you are a man of blood!" Then Abishai son of Zeruiah said to the king, "Why should this dead dog curse my lord the king? Let me go over and cut off his head." But the king said, "What do you and I have in common, you sons of Zeruiah? If he is cursing because the Lord said to him, 'Curse David,' who can ask, 'Why do you do this?'" David then said to Abishai and all his officials, "My son, who is of my own flesh, is trying to take my life. How much more, then, this Benjamite! Leave him alone; let him curse, for the Lord has told him to. It may be that the Lord will see my

distress and repay me with good for the cursing I am receiving today." (2 Samuel 16:5–12)

"For the Lord has told him to;" could you tolerate these types of words from such an unworthy person? Until you can say "Yes," with the Holy Spirit bearing witness to that fact,[4] you will easily be taken in by a man. For you listen to whoever speaks to your flesh, keeps your pride in place, and comes to you on the terms you think you desire. The secret to having ears to hear is a humility that can hear God speak in whatever manner and through whomever He chooses. Do you really want ears to hear?

Hearing Aides

- Why does God give us men to teach us His ways?

- What protects us from false prophets?

- What areas in your life do you not hear from God clearly on and tend to follow men? What areas do you resist following men?

- Ask God for humility to accept correction from others.

Chapter 13

When God Is Silent

Whom have you so dreaded and feared that you have been false to me, and have neither remembered me nor pondered this in your hearts? Is it not because I have long been silent that you do not fear me? (Isaiah 57:11)

When God turns silent we should become very worried and concerned. How sad that many people do not even fear the silence because their hearts are cold and dead. The only time that Jesus felt cut off from the voice of the Father, was when He was crucified on the cross. When Jesus cried, "My God, my God, why have you forsaken me?" our sins which He had taken upon Himself caused something to happen that Jesus had never experienced before. God became silent. The fear of God's silence caused David to pray the following Psalm because he knew that if God remained silent he would "be like those who have gone down to the pit."

> Of David. To you I call, O Lord my Rock; do not turn a deaf ear to me. For if you remain silent, I will be like those who have gone down to the pit. (Psalm 28:1)

Those who do not believe God talks to His children are already doomed because of unbelief.[1] For us, however, who know a living God, realize that when He turns His face from us we are being disciplined. True lovers of God long for the voice of their beloved and when the voice becomes silent, nothing else matters. And we do mean nothing else!

Filling the Silence

The temptation is to try and find another voice to fill the void. Most people begin to mock to themselves the voice of God that they heard before. For this reason, we see failure and sins within the church today. Men take the voice they heard once, refuse to repent when God becomes silent and fill the emptiness with their own voices or the voices of other men. Many do not even realize that God no longer talks to them, but it is the voice of the evil one masking as an angel of light.[2]

Fellowship was broken when our father Adam sinned in the Garden of Eden. God used to come to Adam in the cool of the day to fellowship with him.[3] Jesus Christ came and died so that we might be filled with the righteousness of God, and once again begin to fellowship and hear His voice. For this reason, the writer of Hebrews reminds us that Jesus is the only a source of salvation for those who obey.

> . . . and, once made perfect, he became the source of eternal salvation for all who obey him. (Hebrews 5:9)

Without more holiness, by faith and grace, God cannot and will not talk to us. We must grow into a deeper maturity of holiness. You cannot tell a child things that concern adulthood, but you must wait until the child matures. If however, the child when thirty years old still cannot comprehend adult concepts, something is terribly wrong. This is why Paul declared in 1 Corinthians 3:2, "I gave you milk, not solid food, for you were not yet ready for it. Indeed, you are still not ready." And the writer of Hebrews knew one must wait upon God before moving into new areas of holiness.[4]

God's Discipline

God's will is that we go from strength to strength,[5] growing ever closer in our fellowship with Him until we enter heaven. God only remains silent because we have sinned or because of sinful immaturity. When we act bad and sin, God puts us in the corner to see if we will repent. When He needs to purify us more, God becomes silent to see if our hearts will seek Him and Him alone. One example is found in 2 Chronicles when God left King Hezekiah all alone to "know everything that was in his heart."

> But when envoys were sent by the rulers of Babylon to ask him about the miraculous sign that had occurred in the land, God left him to test him and to know everything that was in his heart. (2 Chronicles 32:31)

Now you might think that God already knows your hearts and that is true. Just as God asked Adam, "Where are you?"[6] when He certainly knew where Adam hid, sin separates us from God. We need to ask ourselves these questions: "What is wrong with me? How have I sinned?" In Adam's case he ate what he should not have and in King Hezekiah's case, pride and not piety had caused him to boast sinfully.[7]

When God becomes silent in your life, it is the time to slow way down, to become very quiet and to wait as long as it takes for Him to speak again. The temptation, however, is to find comfort in something else. It may be a movement of God, a good Christian book, or even in doing something for Him, but if God is not in it then you labor in vain.[8] Do as Isaiah proclaims, wait on the Lord and when He does speak again, accept all that He has to say.

> I will wait for the Lord, who is hiding his face from the house of Jacob. I will put my trust in him. (Isaiah 8:17)

Jesus had the Spirit without limit[9] and fellowshipped continually with God. We on the other hand, at best, stumble[10] in many ways and must undergo painful discipline[11] to have our relationship restored as we mature.

Moments of Silence

Discipline is not always punishment for something done wrong, but also for the purpose of growth. The more we grow in righteousness, the deeper our depth of fellowship with God becomes. As a child grows in wisdom and knowledge, the fellowship between parent and child also grows. We see how God attempted to mature the Israelites as they came out of Egypt through the miracles He performed. The warning for us is that they never learned from their lessons.[12] In between the miracles God performed were moments of relative silence. During these silent times God wanted the Israelites to think on what sins He had revealed to them and for their faith to grow. In other words, God wanted to show them something wicked about themselves so that they could repent and gain a closer fellowship with Him. But alas, they never did learn but whined, moaned, and grumbled to the point it cost them the Promised Land. We too forfeit many promises of God because we do not learn our lessons. In fact, many forfeit Jesus because they remain unwilling to be taught by God. When the Israelites first came out of Egypt, God performed His miracles quickly and closely together. For example, they doubted God would provide water, and without a single rebuke he gave them water.[13] However, when similar situations arose, their faith did not increase, therefore, God began to bring them under judgment.

The same is true for us. Most who come to God at first hear His voice quickly and powerfully. Like He did with the Israelites, God demonstrates that He can be counted on and trusted. However, since we still have so much sin and immaturity, God walks us through the desert to humble us. He grows more quiet and takes longer to perform miracles and to speak to us. During these brief silent times the testing of our heart occurs.

> Remember how the Lord your God led you all the way in the desert these forty years, to humble you and to test you in order to know what was in your heart, whether or not you would keep his commands. (Deuteronomy 8:2)

God, during times of silence, seeks to humble us and to show us our heart. Also during times when God seems far away, although He is always right there, He looks for true faith that trusts in Jesus despite feelings or circumstances. It reveals those who follow Jesus because they love Him and those who selfishly follow Jesus because of the food, rest, peace, and salvation He offers.[14] If we want ears that can hear we must overcome the flesh that seeks a god who blesses our wide gate and wide road.

Hearing Aides

- Why does God grow silent at times?

- Have you experienced the silence of God before? How did you feel during this time?

- How can you make the most of God's silence?

Chapter 14

The Facial Expressions of God

Your eye is the lamp of your body. When your eyes are good, your whole body also is full of light. But when they are bad, your body also is full of darkness. (Luke 11:34)

Not all voices and words come from the mouth. Just as man was created in God's image so we know that He communicates beyond verbal ways. We communicate with the expressions, facial movements, hand gestures, and even in the rising of an eyebrow. Indeed, we communicate with our eyes just as a lamp lights a room. What is inside shines out and communicates things hidden in the soul. So it is with God; the face of God through Jesus communicates volumes. In fact, when we finally die and see Jesus, the Bible tells us we shall be like Him because we see Him face to face.[1]

As a pastor and parent, many times it is not what I say that is important, but what I do not say verbally. Many times my silence communicates more than words. Whether it be unspoken love or rebuke, the voice is clear and resounds more than words. Those that I am closest to in the Lord often sense the love of Christ that flows through me to them by what shines out through my eyes. In the same way, those that are stubborn or rebellious, if they had soft hearts, would know that God is angry and frustrated—not because I rebuke or admonish them, but that my eyes communicate something much more serious than words ever could.

God's Emotions

By seeking the face of God we can grow to become keenly aware of His emotions. As we work out our salvation with fear and trembling, we should become very astute to the emotions of the one we love with all our heart, mind, soul, and strength. If we do this then we can say with the Psalmist, "Blessed are all who take refuge in him" for they know when God smiles and when He frowns. And at the first sign of frowning they run to the mercy seat to repent, for they have learned to "Kiss the Son."

> Kiss the Son, lest he be angry and you be destroyed in your way, for his wrath can flare up in a moment. Blessed are all who take refuge in him. (Psalm 2:12)

Like the burning bush, the majority of God's children are completely unaware of the moods of the Father. How sad that many cannot even hear Jesus sigh deeply, let alone read His face and so never sense the need to repent from the heart.

> He sighed deeply . . . (Mark 8:12)

When we have soft hearts we will hear Jesus speak to us in ways that shatter the soul, or exhilarate the heart. Peter experienced the shattering of the soul. When Peter first heard the call of God to come follow Jesus he fell to his knees in humility.

> When Simon Peter saw this, he fell at Jesus' knees and said, "Go away from me, Lord; I am a sinful man!" (Luke 5:8)

Just a Glance

After many years of following Christ, Peter protested that he would not deny Jesus. Later after his denial, all it took was a glance by Jesus and his soul was shattered. The mark of a soft heart before God is one that just doesn't hear the voice of God and respond, but one that picks up on His ever so subtle moods. As with any mature child, what once required a loud verbal command can be communicated with a glance of the eyes. As with any newlywed couple that at first communicated their love with flowers and grand gestures, in old age can sit together without saying a word and bask in the love God has worked. See how Peter responds to the look of the Lord. Jesus "looked straight at Peter" and he went out and wept "bitterly."

> The Lord turned and looked straight at Peter. Then Peter remembered the word the Lord had spoken to him: "Before the rooster crows today, you will disown me three times." And he went outside and wept bitterly. (Luke 22:61–62)

In the same way, Jesus met Paul on the Damascus road and shouted at him and blinded him. But as their relationship grew deeper, all it took for Paul to feel strengthened in faith was to know Jesus stood at his side.

> But the Lord stood at my side and gave me strength, so that through me the message might be fully proclaimed and all the Gentiles might hear it. And I was delivered from the lion's mouth. (2 Timothy 4:17)

May we all be so blessed that all it takes is for the Lord to stand at our side and give us strength. May we sense His presence and feel courageous, or all we need is a glance to cause us to weep over our sins.

Paul knew the emotions of God and therefore wrote in 2 Corinthians 4:10, "We always carry around in our body the death of Jesus, so that the life of Jesus, may also be revealed in our body." As a believer and disciple of Jesus, I am keenly aware of God's emotions toward me. And He communicates both His displeasure ("the death of Jesus") and His pleasure that I am letting the blood of Jesus do its work, ("the life of Jesus"). I hear much more than words, I feel and sense the emotions of God. Indeed, as He works more righteousness, the working out of His Word occurs more through a quick sense of God's emotion and heart than a bunch of commands. Though I always strive to uphold the commands of God, the face of God communicates much. This is truly seeking the heart of God. When a man seeks the heart of God, hearing not only the voice of God but sensing His facial expressions, he will be granted a heart like David's. A heart that's after God's own heart and obeys everything He asks him to do.

> After removing Saul, he made David their king. He testified concerning him: "I have found David son of Jesse a man after my own heart; he will do everything I want him to do." (Acts 13:22)

HEARING AIDES

- Think of the ways facial expressions and body language effect communication.

- Why is it important to read and understand the emotions of God?

- List some emotions such as love, anger, or disappointment. In what ways can you feel these emotions in God?

- How would understanding the emotions of God help you to hear Him clearer?

Chapter 15

Adulthood— The Spirit of Pentecost

The twelve apostles followed Jesus for many years and stayed with Him all through His trials.

> You are those who have stood by me in my trials. And I confer on you a kingdom, just as my Father conferred one on me. (Luke 22:28–29)

Just as Jesus could give them the kingdom of heaven, if we suffer with Christ we too will have the kingdom conferred on us. Scripture is clear, without sharing in the sufferings of Christ in the world we have no hope of receiving the peace of heaven in the next world.[1] This is not a well accepted doctrine in the church today and, in many circles, stirs up false accusations of preaching salvation by works. We do not wish to enter into that debate here, but want to talk about adulthood in Christ, those who have gained ears that can hear.

Remember, being born again is like human birth. We must be born again and grow up. The Twelve picked up their crosses and followed Jesus all the way to His death on the cross. This truth caused them to die to themselves, learn from their sins, and thus grow up in God. After the resurrection, Jesus breathed on them the Holy Spirit and they became ready to teach others at the day of Pentecost.[2] After all, they died enough to self that Jesus remained alive in them and He could speak with authority through them.[3] Most of their sufferings while following Jesus when He walked the earth matured them, but now after Pentecost they suffered for the sake of others. This demonstrates a true life of selfless love and a sign of adulthood in God.

Selfless Love

Think how selfish a baby behaves at birth. He learns to crawl and stand up all for self. He walks, eats, and plays for himself. Parents have to teach children the virtue of unselfishness. Indeed, the sufferings of an infant's bumping into a table, falling down, and later getting into trouble as a teenager results from their own folly. Only as an adult does selfless love seem to occur when a parent works to provide for the family. Even then we know it is selfish love, for only the cross rids a man of sinful love.

Again, children only focus on themselves and must be taught concern for others. The disciples had learned this, died to self, and could love others as the Holy Spirit directed and empowered them. Paul also let the sufferings of Christ work a death to self that allowed the love of heaven to move through him. Therefore Paul wrote that he endured everything for the sake of others.

> Therefore I endure everything for the sake of the elect, that they too may obtain the salvation that is in Christ Jesus, with eternal glory. (2 Timothy 2:10)

Such selfless love, that does not even follow Jesus for the sake of salvation, was so real that Paul wished he could be sent to hell for the sake of others.[4] When we are dead to self we will be like Christ who literally was cursed for our sakes. This wonderful depth of love comes when we have ears than can hear. Indeed, it is the whole goal of faith.

> The only thing that counts is faith expressing itself through love. (Galatians 5:6b)

The Acts of the Spirit

The book of Acts, from Pentecost on, tells the story of the acts of the Holy Spirit. We tend to think of it as the book of acts of the first Christians, but it's not. It is a book about the voice of God moving and empowering those who truly believe in Jesus.

From tongues of fire, to the death of Ananias and Sapphira, we see the Holy Spirit speaking and moving in the lives of all who had ears to hear. The Holy Spirit could easily communicate God's will. In the following passage, we see disciples who had ears to hear. They did not seek anything special from the Lord. In the middle of worshipping God they heard the Holy Spirit's voice say, "Set apart . . ."

> While they were worshiping the Lord and fasting, the Holy Spirit said, "Set apart for me Barnabas and Saul for the work to which I have called them." (Acts 13:2)

The book of Acts is not the story of church committees planning acts for God; nor the story of man's wisdom striving to increase church membership. Never is the book of Acts about man. It is about the voice of the Holy Spirit. Look at the following Scripture and you will see the Holy

Spirit intimately directing when, how, and in what ways a man should be evangelized.

> So he started out, and on his way he met an Ethiopian eunuch, an important official in charge of all the treasury of Candace, queen of the Ethiopians. This man had gone to Jerusalem to worship, and on his way home was sitting in his chariot reading the book of Isaiah the prophet. The Spirit told Philip, "Go to that chariot and stay near it." Then Philip ran up to the chariot and heard the man reading Isaiah the prophet. "Do you understand what you are reading?" Philip asked. (Acts 8:27–30)

"The Spirit told Philip, 'Go to that chariot and stay near it.'" The Holy Spirit's voice was clear and to the point—"that chariot," not some other chariot. The Spirit told Philip to just "stay near it" and wait to see what the Lord would direct next. Immediately in obedience to that voice, Philip went with the mind of Christ and began to share the gospel. This speaking by the Holy Spirit did not occur to make Philip feel special, but to fulfill a very serious work in the humility of Christ. The question is, are we willing to go onto maturity so that we are available for the Holy Spirit to move and speak to us? Like Peter, are we so dead to our own plans that when we hear the Holy Spirit tell us to "go downstairs" and "not hesitate," will we trust Jesus and obey?

> While Peter was still thinking about the vision, the Spirit said to him, "Simon, three men are looking for you. So get up and go downstairs. Do not hesitate to go with them, for I have sent them." (Acts 10:19–20)

Reaching Adulthood

Can we trust God even when the Holy Spirit warns us that we are about to suffer? Do we really want to hear the Holy Spirit tell us such things? Remember, Jesus went to the cross knowing that it was the Father's will.[5] Jesus could hear God clearly and prayed until He could submit with joy. In the same way, are you honestly willing to hear both the good and bad that God has planned for your life? Of course we use bad in a human sense, because everything God plans and speaks to us is for our good, even when it hurts. Could we hear what Paul heard and rejoice?

> I only know that in every city the Holy Spirit warns me that prison and hardships are facing me. (Acts 20:23)

Most people in the church today are unwilling to listen to the Holy Spirit. Indeed, they cannot even get past the sermons I preach because it offends and they don't like the tone. Few can give up their lives enough for God to hear the voice of the Holy Spirit. Pentecost is the spirit of maturity in "adult" disciples' lives. They have grown up and are willing to listen to the Holy Spirit and joyfully obey that voice. They have learned to distinguish the voice of the Holy Spirit from others. They know which voice to run from and which to run toward. Blessed are those who have matured unto adulthood in Jesus Christ. Those who have ears to hear allow the Holy Spirit to work a life of true heavenly inspired selfless love for others.

Hearing Aides

- What transformation took place in the apostles after Pentecost?

- What is the real purpose for hearing God?

- List some things you resist in hearing from God. Take one thing on your list and ask God to help you to have a willing heart to obey.

Chapter 16

Judgment and Judging

One of the greatest sins and weaknesses in the church today is judging. We far too quickly declare, "Oh, they have a good heart in the Lord," or more often, we pronounce a judgment like, "They are wicked and full of sin." To make any judgment, whether good or bad, is a sin if we have not heard from God to declare that judgment. Jesus could judge without being judgmental because He did not judge, but spoke judgements only as He heard God speak them. Jesus was not the judge, only the messenger.

> By myself I can do nothing; I judge only as I hear, and my judgment is just, for I seek not to please myself but him who sent me. (John 5:30)

We too must learn to shut up and only speak a word of judgement as we "hear" from God. And if we do not hear anything about anyone or about a situation, we should not utter or think anything about it. We have hinted through this book that only a fool delights in airing his opinion, let us now look directly at the Scripture.

> A fool finds no pleasure in understanding but delights in airing his own opinions. (Proverbs 18:2)

When we feel good about stating our judgments, whether the judgment is good or bad, we play the fool. God sees us as a fool. Indeed, the angels and the saints who have died no doubt shake their heads in dismay. They have beheld the holiness of God and cannot believe we so quickly voice our opinions as judgments. Indeed, we should know that even the archangel Michael did not say more than God commanded him to declare. But how quickly we speak without first listening to God.

> But even the archangel Michael, when he was disputing with the devil about the body of Moses, did not dare to bring a slanderous accusation against him, but said, "The Lord rebuke you!" (Jude 1:9)

God is the only one pure enough to make any judgment and when we speak on our own we tell God we are wiser than He. Often when by the Spirit we point out the sin in a situation, someone will respond by saying, "Oh, I know they love the Lord, they have a good heart." Such statements are full of pride, unless we hear God tell us that the person has a good heart. In the following passage John could declare the truth about a fellow believer because the Holy Spirit, which is the spirit of truth, testified that his good evaluation of another was confirmed by God. John only repeated what he heard from the Holy Spirit.[1]

> Demetrius is well spoken of by everyone—and even by the truth itself. We also speak well of him, and you know that our testimony is true. (3 John 1:12)

John was mature, full of the Holy Spirit, and had enough of the cross in his life to put to death his opinions about others. Therefore he could say, "and you know that our testimony is true."

Right Judgments

We must speak judgments only as the Holy Spirit directs and in order to hear those directions we must be crucified to our thoughts. For this reason Peter could judge the heart of a couple in the first church. Yes, only God knows the heart of each person, but clearly God reveals those hearts to those who can hear Him speak. Peter could say to Ananias, "How is it that Satan has so filled your heart?" because God spoke to Peter and revealed the man's heart.

> Then Peter said, "Ananias, how is it that Satan has so filled your heart that you have lied to the Holy Spirit and have kept for yourself some of the money you received for the land?" (Acts 5:3)

As Jesus points out in the following passage, we "judge by human standards" and with our sinful eyes and ears. We measure things by outward appearance and so always make wrong judgments. We must "stop" our judging and learn how to make a "right judgment."

> Stop judging by mere appearances, and make a right judgment. (John 7:24)

Therefore, any judgment we make, good or bad, correct or incorrect, is at best stained deeply with sin. We typically judge others as good, or not so bad, if we like them or if they are similar to us in nature. We judge others as evil if we don't personally like their actions.

> You judge by human standards; I pass judgment on no one. But if I do judge, my decisions are right, because I am not alone. I stand with the Father, who sent me. (John 8:15–16)

Hearing from God

When we judge, we stand alone. Jesus, however, never stood alone because He only repeated what the Father told Him, and therefore could say "I stand with the Father." We should be like Jesus that passes judgment on no one and wait for the Father to give us His insight and judgments on every issue. Likewise, Paul taught that the spiritual man makes judgments about all things.[2] For the spiritual man listens to the Holy Spirit before ever making a judgment on anything or anyone. When we are dead enough to self to say "I stand with the Father" then we can make judgments. In reality, we do not make the judgment, rather, we hear from God about His judgments and merely rely on His verdict. Jesus walked with this spirit of humility, as should we.

> I have much to say in judgment of you. But he who sent me is reliable, and what I have heard from him I tell the world. (John 8:26)

Whatever Jesus "heard from" God, He told the world. Jesus never offered His opinion or thoughts on any matter, but only repeated what God spoke to Him. And if we do not hear God's clear voice in a judgment we should walk with great humility and fear. Many things are simply not our business[3] and we should judge nothing before the appointed time by God.[4]

"Paul, filled with the Holy Spirit" spoke some powerful judgmental words. Most Christian circles today would condemn Paul as unloving, but he judged without being judgmental as Jesus commanded.[5] Paul could do this because he was not the one doing the judging. God judged through Paul and he understood the judgment because he could hear the Father's voice. Paul could judge Elymas and call him "a child of the devil" because, like Jesus, Paul heard the voice of God.

> But Elymas the sorcerer (for that is what his name means) opposed them and tried to turn the proconsul from the faith. Then Saul, who was also called Paul, filled with the Holy Spirit, looked straight at Elymas and said, "You are a child of the devil and an enemy of everything that is right! You are full of all kinds of deceit and trickery. Will you never stop perverting the right ways of the Lord? Now the hand of the Lord is against you. You are going to be blind, and for a time you will be unable to see the light of the sun." Immediately mist and darkness came over him, and he groped about, seeking someone to lead him by the hand. When the proconsul saw what had happened, he believed, for he was amazed at the teaching about the Lord. (Acts 13:8–12)

Our Christianity remains so powerless today and so full of unloving, self-righteous judgments because we are not dead enough to our opinions to hear from God the truth. Again the vast majority of the time, most things are none of our business, but when God makes them our business we dare not open our mouths to voice a judgment unless we have heard from the Father "what" to say and "how" to say it.

> For I did not speak of my own accord, but the Father who sent me commanded me *what* to say and *how* to say it. I know that his command leads to eternal life. So whatever I say is just what the Father has told me to say." (John 12:49–50, emphasis added)

This is the nature of eternal life; to only say "what the Father has told" us to say. When we speak on our own we slander even if we are correct, for we play God and have sought to remove Him from His throne. How sad to contemplate the many lives ruined because we don't have ears to hear God's voice before declaring a judgment.

Hearing Aides

- What causes someone to act like a fool?

- Why is it dangerous to make judgments—good or bad?

- List some "human standards" we tend to make judgments by. How would this change if we made judgments by the Spirit?

Chapter 17

God's Voice and Conviction of Sin

> But when he, the Spirit of truth, comes, he will guide you into all truth. He will not speak on his own; he will speak only what he hears, and he will tell you what is yet to come. (John 16:13)

Truly there is no condemnation in Christ, but there is conviction in Christ. Being filled with the Holy Spirit means we are filled with a "Spirit of truth." Indeed, the Holy Spirit will speak only what he hears and will guide us "into all truth." Since we are, by nature, totally vile and wicked[1] a battle wages in our souls. The Spirit of Truth tries to speak truth to us who naturally listen to lies. Man in his sinful nature upon first hearing the truth thinks it is a lie, because it is not his natural language. This is why so many people look for churches where they feel comfortable and miss salvation, for we are comfortable with lies. Most people who consider coming to the church where I pastor don't like it at first. Even with all the love and joy it is not always comfortable because the Holy Spirit with His truth speaks to them things they do not want to hear. They think the truth is a foreign language and are often afraid at first. Paul writes of this battle in Galatians.

> For the sinful nature desires what is contrary to the Spirit, and the Spirit what is contrary to the sinful nature. They are in conflict with each other, so that you do not do what you want. (Galatians 5:17)

A "conflict" takes place. The Holy Spirit speaks the truth and our sinful nature says, "No it is a lie." To further intensify the battle, Satan whispers to us that the truth we hear from the Holy Spirit is indeed a lie. Those that listen to the Holy Spirit and believe what Jesus says, will choose to do what they don't want to do. The very heart of the message of the cross is doing what we do not want to do. False Christianity allows you to do what you want and to obey your own voice.

It should not surprise us that we often feel convicted of sin because the sinful nature always wants to live the lie sin offers. In order to have more of the Holy Spirit, guiding us into deeper truth, we must often feel convicted of what is wrong. And to keep us from going back to our lies the Holy Spirit must convict us by reminding us of the real truth.

Often two extremes occur with conviction. There are those who will not listen to any conviction because they call it condemnation from the Devil, and then there are those who listen to every voice concerning sin in their lives. Both lead to ruin. We should listen to the Holy Spirit convicting us in the smallest of details in our lives,[2] but we should also know which voices to ignore.

Satan's Voice

Let us look at and listen to one of the greatest lies Satan tells the church today that costs millions true salvation in

Jesus. Because the Devil lost to Scripture when tempting Jesus, he tried to quote Scripture to Jesus. In other words, the Devil tried to use Scripture to get Jesus to sin.

> Then the devil took him to the holy city and had him stand on the highest point of the temple. "If you are the Son of God," he said, "throw yourself down. For it is written: "'He will command his angels concerning you, and they will lift you up in their hands, so that you will not strike your foot against a stone.'" Jesus answered him, "It is also written: 'Do not put the Lord your God to the test.'" (Matthew 4:5–7)

The Devil quoted Psalm 91:11–12 and he quoted it in context. There was nothing tricky about the Scripture Satan used, except it was Satan who quoted it, and therein lies the danger. The Scripture was true but it did not come from the Holy Spirit, and therefore powerless and poisonous. For this reason, the Bible declares that no one can really say "'Jesus is Lord,' except by the Holy Spirit."[3] Lots of individuals can and do declare that Jesus is Lord, but there is no real truth in it and they are not saved. Satan has lifted up the church to the "highest point of the temple" and quotes verses about God's love and concern for them. And in the mist of quoting Scriptures about God's love, Satan bids them to jump off. They are after all, children of the King and loved by Him. How many today obey the voice of Satan as he quotes Scripture to their everlasting destruction. So many upon their death beds hear Satan quoting them the Scriptures.

Men often speak against my preaching and judge my character as evil. Sometimes they are even correct about a fault or sin in my life. Indeed, the Devil knows my sins all too well and when he speaks to me about them I can only conclude he is correct. Of course, many other times men lie about my character and so does Satan. What is the solution to this dilemma? What we have been saying all along. We must come to recognize the Shepherd's voice and to submit to that voice's conviction of sin. Let's look at a biblical example.

> David said to Gad, "I am in deep distress. Let us fall into the hands of the Lord, for his mercy is great; but do not let me fall into the hands of men." (2 Samuel 24:14)

God still had to discipline David and punish him for his sins. But David knew better than to submit to wicked men.

Accepting Conviction

Do not sin by refusing conviction when God strikes hard against your sin. On the other hand, do not accept any judgment that does not have the Holy Spirit in it, even if the accusers quote Scripture. Do not even listen to yourself quoting Scriptures about your life, but let the Holy Spirit speak and guide. The Holy Spirit is your counselor, so listen to the counsel He speaks.[4]

Finally, let me share with you one tactic to use in spiritual warfare. Assume that every judgment a man brings against you is true. Assume that everything the Devil speaks against you is true. Assume all those things with a pure heart, looking for signs of sin, evil motives, and actions that prove such judgments to be true. Do that, but run immediately to the Lord with an honest desire to repent. Satan certainly will not often speak to you about your sins because he does not want you running to God. And when men point out faults and sins and you run to God for a changed life, you will thank them for they have done you a favor. In all that you do, seek out and listen for the voice of the Holy Spirit, the Spirit of Truth. Do this and "the God of peace" will "sanctify you through and through" by the conviction of what is Truth.

> May God himself, the God of peace, sanctify you through and through. May your whole spirit, soul and body be kept blameless at the coming of our Lord Jesus Christ. The one who calls you is faithful and he will do it. (1 Thessalonians 5:23–24)

Hearing Aides

- Explain the difference between condemnation and conviction.

- Why do you think that we tend to want to believe lies?

- How have you experienced the two extremes of conviction in your life?

- Are there areas in your life that you feel that someone has misjudged you? Take some time to hear from the Lord and allow Him to convict you of the Truth.

Chapter 18

The Fruit of Old Age

The good fruit of old age causes a disciple to hear God very loud and clear. John, an older man by the time of Revelation, because of the Word of God and the sufferings in Christ, was exiled on the Island of Patmos. Whether on an island or not, we become more isolated from the world with each passing year, if we are true disciples of Jesus who live as strangers in this world.[1]

> I, John, your brother and companion in the suffering and kingdom and patient endurance that are ours in Jesus, was on the island of Patmos because of the word of God and the testimony of Jesus. On the Lord's Day I was in the Spirit, and I heard behind me a loud voice like a trumpet. (Revelation 1:9–10)

Those who have given up all for Jesus can enjoy sweet fellowship with God. When the flesh doesn't have to be doing something, lusts are tamed, and appetites made obedient with self control, what rest is theirs in Christ. Like

John, we become dead to the world and we will hear the "loud voice" of the Lord. The more deafened we are to the world the more the voice of the Lord will resound like a "trumpet" in ears that can hear.

Like Paul, at this stage we will know that we are ready to meet the living God on good terms.[2] Not in presumptuous faith like most,[3] but because we have remained faithful as the cross worked death to self in us. Faith inspired by grace, rather than the belief of man, will work a freedom where the Holy Spirit can speak clearly that it is time to die joyfully in Jesus. Because Paul followed the voice of the Holy Spirit to pour himself out for the sake of others, that same Holy Spirit assured him it was time to die and what awaited him.

> For I am already being poured out like a drink offering, and the time has come for my departure. I have fought the good fight, I have finished the race, I have kept the faith. Now there is in store for me the crown of righteousness, which the Lord, the righteous Judge, will award to me on that day—and not only to me, but also to all who have longed for his appearing. (2 Timothy 4:6–8)

Peter likewise knew from the Lord that it was almost time to die because he had been a "drink offering" to others. And Jesus said that God would always honor those who serve Him.[4] How true it is that Jesus leaves none who have true faith as orphans. When He speaks His voice guides, protects, empowers, rebukes, comforts, enlightens, and makes clear His plans for us.

> . . . because I know that I will soon put it aside, as our Lord Jesus Christ has made clear to me. (2 Peter 1:14)

Going Home

Not all of God's children will live to an old age, yet many still hear the voice of God calling them home. Some may even go home raptured by visions of God's power amidst the sufferings of Christ as Stephen did.[5] Others of us may pass through darker valleys when God hides His face and silences His voice as we die. Let them count it as joyful discipline.

Still others may be taken in an instant through accidents and failure of our bodies, but let all who honestly have taken up their cross, denied self, and followed the voice of God have rich faith. God is merciful and knows how each of us should die. He will not let us be tempted beyond what we can bear[6] and however we die, it is meant to rid us of sin and self and to bring us into God's righteousness and holiness.[7] Just listen for the voice that tells you it is almost time. And if God seeks to make you afraid of Him don't argue Scripture back at the Holy Spirit, submit and trust even when God slays you.[8]

The Lord seeks to speak to many, but they quote their favorite Scripture and try to rebuke Him with it. As a result, God will just shut up toward such people and leave them with their own voices and a Christian belief that is a lie. I often shut up when trying to bless[9] someone with a Scripture when they refuse to repent and retaliate by quoting me a Scripture about God's love.

Let us learn our lessons, soften our hearts, and open wide our souls even near death, for "precious in the sight of the Lord is the death of his saints." (Psalm 116:15). Let those who die young in the Lord be like the good thief on the cross, asking nothing more than for Jesus to remember them. Let us not be like the other thief that wanted deliverance from the message of the cross.

All Will Hear

Children are amazed by the most basic of things about life, but as we mature we can glory in the wisdom of daily life. In the same way, as we grow up in the Lord, we at first struggle to believe that God actually talks to us today. As we mature, however, we marvel at the wisdom of Him who has spoken so often to us. "Now" has "come" the time when we who are dead in our sins hear God and are alive because we hear the voice of the Holy Spirit.[10]

> I tell you the truth, a time is coming and has now come when the dead will hear the voice of the Son of God and those who hear will live. (John 5:25)

For this reason, Jesus told us not to be amazed, that is, not to even bother asking the question, "Does God speak to us today?" For Jesus tells us that not only does God speak to those who obey, but a time is coming when everyone will hear the voice of God.

> Do not be amazed at this, for a time is coming when all who are in their graves will hear his voice and come out—those who have done good will rise to live, and those who have done evil will rise to be condemned. (John 5:28–29)

We, as God's children, at first feel amazed that He talks to us, but when we grow old in Jesus we will not only hear His voice but also His trumpets and more. We will see Jesus face to face, see His emotions and hear His lips speak more clearly than we have ever heard a human speak.

> Now we see but a poor reflection as in a mirror; then we shall see face to face. Now I know in part; then I shall know fully, even as I am fully known. (1 Corinthians 13:12)

Here in this world we hear but a faint whisper of God. Even when He shouts and His voice breaks the cedars of Lebanon,[11] it is but a whisper of what is to come. As Job records, "faint" is the "whisper we hear of him."

> And these are but the outer fringe of his works; how faint the whisper we hear of him! Who then can understand the thunder of his power? (Job 26:14)

May God give us ears to hear that faint whisper in our daily life. In our old age, even though we might grow physically deaf, God's whisper will become clearer and clearer. And when He speaks, we will have ears that can hear no matter how faint His voice might be.

HEARING AIDES

- What can we look forward to as believers in Christ?

- What are the benefits of maturity?

- Do you fear death? Draw nearer to God in order to hear His voice of comfort.

Chapter 19

First Step—Laying a Foundation

> The rain came down, the streams rose, and the winds blew and beat against that house; yet it did not fall, because it had its foundation on the rock. But everyone who hears these words of mine and does not put them into practice is like a foolish man who built his house on sand. (Matthew 7:25–26)

Jesus said, "But everyone who hears these words" and does not lay a foundation on rock is foolish indeed. So, how does someone get started hearing God? How does one lay a foundation on rock? How can a foundation be laid that will not end in deceiving ourselves about the voice we think we heard?

First of all, a foundation of rock is hard. It takes hard work to build upon the rock Jesus Christ. Quick easy answers to hearing God are sand and end in the destruction of those who build upon it. Everyone looks for a church where they feel comfortable and they do the same with hearing God's voice. We want it easy and simple, but wrestling with our flesh to hear God correctly will require tedious work. Day in and day out a man will have to dig into rock, sweating, and working until the foundation is thoroughly laid. It is boring work, often doing the same thing day after day until the foundation is dug. To read only Scripture without imposing any explanation, understanding, or church dogma is tough, tedious work, especially when our flesh would love to do something more exciting. This is why so many churches seek excitement—they feel bored with the Lord.

Only after the foundations is laid can any thought be given to building the actual house. Being crucified to self is not comfortable and periods of confusion and perplexity accompany anyone trying to hear God's voice correctly. Like Paul, you will feel tempted to despair. God will seek to keep you weak though the cross, a very unpleasurable thing to endure.

> We are hard pressed on every side, but not crushed; perplexed, but not in despair. (2 Corinthians 4:8)

Full Surrender

One of the first questions you need to ask yourself is, "Do I really want to hear God's voice?" If so, then start with Romans 12.

> Therefore, I urge you, brothers, in view of God's mercy, to offer your bodies as living sacrifices, holy and pleasing to God—this is your spiritual act of worship. Do not conform any longer to the pattern of this world, but be transformed by the renewing of your mind. Then you will be able to test and approve what God's will is—his good, pleasing and perfect will. (Romans 12:1–2)

Go quietly into your prayer closet, or in the secret place of your heart, and offer your body as a living sacrifice to

God. Tell Him it is His to do with as He pleases. You will arise, sleep, give, work, love, labor, and everything else done in the body only at the leading of His Holy Spirit. Tell Him you will listen for His voice only and do all that voice calls you to do. That you will learn the lessons He seeks to teach you and hate your life for His sake. Paul tells us this is an honest act of spiritual worship. Anything less is a man worshipping an idol he has made. An idol named "Jesus" but it still an idol nevertheless. Only those who listen to God, offering their bodies, have ears to hear.

Paul said that we should no longer follow the "pattern of this world." We cannot discuss all the patterns of the world here, but we will touch on a few. One of the main patterns of the world is to make excuses for our sin. Everyone has excuses why they do not obey God. Those who honestly desire to follow Him must crucify all excuses. You can't say, "I don't have the money," or "The situation just didn't allow it." In all that Jesus did, He rose above the excuses and the demands of life and followed God's will. When 5,000 needed food, Jesus fed them. He didn't say, "Oh, it is not in my food budget to do it." When God called Jesus to leave all, He left. He didn't say, "First let me go and say good-bye to my family." It is never convenient to do God's will. Never! The Evil One controls this world, and he will never make it easy to obey God. Christians in this world will always be required to make bricks without straw.[1]

Paul said, "let your mind be transformed." Our way of thinking, things we meditate on, all that involves our mind and motives must be transformed by the Holy Spirit. From, how we read and understand Scripture to eating dinner,[2] must be transformed and made different. We must gain a heavenly mind from God if we want to have ears that can hear heavenly things spoken to us. Like children that must be taught what everything means, what words mean and even how to reason and think, so too, it will take many years for God to transform our minds.

Only after this foundation has been laid will you be "able to test and approve what God's will is—his good, pleasing and perfect will." This is why so many do not have ears to hear. Since they haven't done this, when someone speaks what Scripture really means or what God requires, the Lord's will becomes anything but good, pleasing and perfect. Indeed, such people cannot take pleasure in what the Holy Spirit speaks to them because they have not offered themselves to God 100% and waited upon Him to transform their minds. Those who offer their bodies to the Lord, for Him to do as He wills, will be given ears that can hear.

Hearing Aides

- What is the foundation we must build on if we want to hear God?

- Romans 12 tells us that we know the will of God by becoming living sacrifices. List some things in your life you know you need to sacrifice.

- What patterns of this world do you still follow? Ask God to crucify these things in your life.

Chapter 20

Cord of Three—A Summary

. . . A cord of three strands is not quickly broken. (Ecclesiastes 4:12b)

We have by no means discovered all the different ways God speaks. We have however, laid a foundation on which you can build upon.

We have looked at the three cords of having ears to hear. One, faith, two, the cross and three, obedience. If any of these three are missing, then the rope will weaken and the danger of breaking increases. For example, one may have faith that God speaks. But without picking up the painful cross of Christ with a heart ready to joyfully obey God, you find immature and disobedient children, more enthralled with spiritual gifts than true faith. In the end, they will either go to hell or be one of the few that escape through the flames.[1] On the other hand, if someone does not have the faith to believe that God talks today, but seeks to pick up a cross and obey the Bible, they will become Pharisees, self-righteous and puffed up, twice as fit for hell.

The five rules for hearing God's voice are:

- There are no principles
- There are no laws.
- There are no steps.
- There are no guidelines.
- There are no rules.

There is only the message of the cross that, if accepted, has the power to crucify a man to his own voice, the voice of other men, the voice of the world, and ultimately the voice of Satan which has taken captive the world. If you meet a man, read a book, or hear a sermon that tells you they understand how to hear God's voice apart from the cross, then run from them immediately. If you hear a message that has reduced the message of the cross down to steps, stages or principles, then turn a deaf ear.

If you think you understand how to hear God's voice, that you have the principles down, then you do not clearly understand anything about hearing God's voice. The "man who thinks he knows something" about how to hear God does not yet understand as he should.

> The man who thinks he knows something does not yet know as he ought to know. But the man who loves God is known by God. (1 Corinthians 8:2–3)

In short, man is powerless to understand how to gain ears to hear. He can study, pray, and examine the Greek and Hebrew all day long and that will not give him ears that can hear. You cannot commit suicide by crucifixion and gaining ears that can hear is totally a work of the Holy Spirit. If you think you know "something" about this business of hearing God, then you do "not yet know as" you ought to know. For knowing is only gained by being known by God.[2]

Meaningless Talk

All you can do is offer yourself to God and let Him do the work of teaching you how to have ears to hear. But the more unteachable you become, the more you refuse to move on, the less you are willing to be corrected, the greater the danger you will live a deceived Christian life. The more you refuse to accept the painful, offensive message of the cross, the more likely you will follow the deceptive words of man that comes in the name of the Lord. Paul warned young Timothy about this. Many preachers can teach this but because they do not have a pure heart, good conscience, and a sincere faith, they only preach meaningless talk.

> The goal of this command is love, which comes from a pure heart and a good conscience and a sincere faith. Some have wandered away from these and turned to meaningless talk. (1 Timothy 1:5–6)

If the basis of true love for God, which we have looked in this short book, is not present in a church, then their Christianity is just meaningless talk. While most rebel against ever accepting the message of the cross, many more slowly wander from it. In other words, little by little, with every correction refused, every call to deny self rejected and every demand for more faith ignored, they slowly move off the narrow road.

Coming Closer to the Cross

Think of Jesus. As He followed the voice of the Lord, it led more and more toward the sufferings of the cross. The same is true with us. The more God talks to us, the more He will take us closer to the cross. You will feel and know the cross that crucifies self, exposes more sin, works more humility and shares more in the sufferings of Christ. If this is not present in the voice you hear or in the sermons you listen to about hearing God's voice, then you hear a lie. If any book, magazine article, or publication does not point you to the sufferings of Christ then it is not offering you the truth about hearing God's voice. You will never gain ears that can hear and should turn away from such things. In the Scripture below we see Paul talking about the sufferings and the resurrection of Christ.

> I want to know Christ and the power of his resurrection and the fellowship of sharing in his sufferings, becoming like him in his death, and so, somehow, to attain to the resurrection from the dead. Not that I have already obtained all this, or have already been made perfect, but I press on to take hold of that for which Christ Jesus took hold of me. (Philippians 3:10–12)

Paul declared, "I want," but do we really want? Do we want the suffering of Christ that will give us fellowship with Jesus? Is it little wonder that God does not talk to most people? They do not suffer, out of love for the sake of others, but remain selfish brats that like living in the household but do not love the homeowner.

And did Paul shy away from the sufferings of Christ? By no means! Paul admitted he has not "obtained all" of this or been made perfect, but he did something we seldom see in the church today. Paul pressed on to take hold of the things of God. If we want ears that can hear, then we must press on in the sufferings of Christ with the cross God will give us.

This does not mean we go out today and seek to inflict painful sufferings on ourselves.[3] It means that we listen for the voice of the Holy Spirit to guide us in and through sufferings. It means we never feel surprised that in order to hear God's voice correctly we must suffer against sin.[4] Peter was clear on this. Only those who suffer in their bodies are done with sin. As a "result" they have ears that can hear and can know and do the will of God.

> Therefore, since Christ suffered in his body, arm yourselves also with the same attitude, because he who has suffered in his body is done with sin. As a result, he does not live the rest of his earthly life for evil human desires, but rather for the will of God. (1 Peter 4:1–2)

The Groan Test

Finally, the acid test to discerning God's voice is the burden, the groan test. If the burden and groaning are missing, then odds are you do not hear the voice of the Lord. When we are free from concern about our flesh when doing the Lord's will, we have put down the cross and live a lie. We always will wrestle in our flesh in order to hear His voice. As the Scripture below tells us, God gives us His Spirit "as a deposit, guaranteeing what is to come." This promise and the Spirit, fill us with great joy. But with this joy we groan and feel burdened. If the groaning and burden of the cross are not present, yet I claim to be filled with the joy of the Holy Spirit, I am not in the Spirit, and do not hear God's voice.

> Meanwhile we groan, longing to be clothed with our heavenly dwelling, because when we are clothed, we will

> not be found naked. For while we are in this tent, we groan and are burdened, because we do not wish to be unclothed but to be clothed with our heavenly dwelling, so that what is mortal may be swallowed up by life. Now it is God who has made us for this very purpose and has given us the Spirit as a deposit, guaranteeing what is to come. (2 Corinthians 5:2–5)

Groaning and feeling the burden, like crucifixion, is uncomfortable, and everyone wants to feel comfortable. But if the universe itself feels burdened, we as disciples of Jesus should not for a moment think we will escape. This makes us ready to hear God's voice and purifies our hearts. For example, as a pastor, individuals give money to the church. As I use that money I feel the weight of a burden and groan under the possibility that I could be like Judas and use that money to please myself. This testing and battling to make sure that my heart remains pure, allows me to hear God's voice so that He can direct me into His will concerning the money. If this burden were not present, if I do not realize this possibility and groan under it, then I am doomed to commit the sin. For the Holy Spirit speaks two things at the same time. One, to use the money to preach the gospel, and two, not to be like Judas and trade my Savior for a few coins. I rejoice in the gift given and am very sober in its use.[5] I desire to become like Paul, who was sorrowful, yet always rejoicing[6] and always carrying around the death of Jesus that he might also have the life of Christ in him.[7]

If you want ears that can hear, the fruit of a resurrected life, then deny yourself, pick up your cross and follow Jesus.[8] To those who do so, God always gives ears that can hear His voice.

Hearing Aides

- Why are there no rules or principles to hearing God's voice?

- Put your life through the moan and groan test. Do you groan for more of God's will in your life?

- In what areas do you need to suffer more so that you can hear God?

- Tie the cord of faith, the cross, and surrender to the work of the Spirit to gain ears to hear.

Everything Said

May our hearts be awake listening for the voice of our lover. Let us listen for His knock and voice.

> I slept but my heart was awake. Listen! My lover is knocking: "Open to me, my sister, my darling, my dove, my flawless one. My head is drenched with dew, my hair with the dampness of the night." (Song of Songs 5:2)

Endnotes

Chapter 1: The Voice of God

1. Psalm 19:1–4 For the director of music. A psalm of David. The heavens declare the glory of God; the skies proclaim the work of his hands. Day after day they pour forth speech; night after night they display knowledge. There is no speech or language where their voice is not heard. Their voice goes out into all the earth, their words to the ends of the world. In the heavens he has pitched a tent for the sun,
2. Colossians 3:2 Set your minds on things above, not on earthly things.
3. Jeremiah 23:36 But you must not mention "the oracle of the Lord" again, because every man's own word becomes his oracle and so you distort the words of the living God, the Lord Almighty, our God.
4. Jeremiah 17:9 The heart is deceitful above all things and beyond cure. Who can understand it?
5. 1 Corinthians 2:2 For I resolved to know nothing while I was with you except Jesus Christ and him crucified.
6. *Hating for Jesus,* by Timothy Williams, ISBN 1-57921-646-3

Chapter 2: The Burning Bush

1. Luke 19:44 They will dash you to the ground, you and the children within your walls. They will not leave one stone on another, because you did not recognize the time of God's coming to you.
2. Job 37:6–7 He says to the snow, "Fall on the earth," and to the rain shower, "Be a mighty downpour." So that all men he has made may know his work, he stops every man from his labor.
3. Genesis 28:16 When Jacob awoke from his sleep, he thought, "Surely the Lord is in this place, and I was not aware of it."
4. Luke 21:34 Be careful, or your hearts will be weighed down with dissipation, drunkenness and the anxieties of life, and that day will close on you unexpectedly like a trap.
5. 2 Samuel 7:18 Then King David went in and sat before the Lord, and he said: "Who am I, O Sovereign Lord, and what is my family, that you have brought me this far?"
6. Mark 6:4 Jesus said to them, "Only in his hometown, among his relatives and in his own house is a prophet without honor."
7. Romans 1:5 Through him and for his name's sake, we received grace and apostleship to call people from among all the Gentiles to the obedience that comes from faith.
8. Exodus 4:24 At a lodging place on the way, the Lord met Moses and was about to kill him.
9. Ecclesiastes 5:2 Do not be quick with your mouth, do not be hasty in your heart to utter anything before God. God is in heaven and you are on earth, so let your words be few.
10. Matthew 6:7 And when you pray, do not keep babbling like pagans, for they think they will be heard because of their many words.
11. Hebrews 4:9–10 There remains, then, a Sabbath-rest for the people of God; for anyone who enters God's rest also rests from his own work, just as God did from his.
12. Exodus 34:28 Moses was there with the Lord forty days and forty nights without eating bread or drinking water. And he wrote on the tablets the words of the covenant—the Ten Commandments.

Chapter 3: The Sin of Unbelief

1. Psalm 19:1–3 The heavens declare the glory of God; the skies proclaim the work of his hands. Day after day they pour forth speech; night after night they display knowledge. There is no speech or language where their voice is not heard.

2. John 8:43–44 Why is my language not clear to you? Because you are unable to hear what I say. You belong to your father, the devil, and you want to carry out your father's desire. He was a murderer from the beginning, not holding to the truth, for there is no truth in him. When he lies, he speaks his native language, for he is a liar and the father of lies.
3. Matthew 24:12 Because of the increase of wickedness, the love of most will grow cold,
4. Isaiah 5:20 Woe to those who call evil good and good evil, who put darkness for light and light for darkness, who put bitter for sweet and sweet for bitter.
5. 1 John 2:6 Whoever claims to live in him must walk as Jesus did.
6. John 5:38 nor does his word dwell in you, for you do not believe the one he sent.
7. *Eau de Cult,* by Timothy Williams, ISBN 1-57921-511-4

Chapter 4: The Promised Land

1. Romans 1:5 Through him and for his name's sake, we received grace and apostleship to call people from among all the Gentiles to the obedience that comes from faith.
2. Numbers 14:44 Nevertheless, in their presumption they went up toward the high hill country, though neither Moses nor the ark of the Lord's covenant moved from the camp.
3. Exodus 20:25 If you make an altar of stones for me, do not build it with dressed stones, for you will defile it if you use a tool on it.
4. Ephesians 5:17 Therefore do not be foolish, but understand what the Lord's will is.
5. 1 John 2:6 Whoever claims to live in him must walk as Jesus did.
6. John 14:16–17 And I will ask the Father, and he will give you another Counselor to be with you forever—the Spirit of truth . . .
7. Psalm 29:5 The voice of the Lord breaks the cedars; the Lord breaks in pieces the cedars of Lebanon.
8. John 5:39–40 You diligently study the Scriptures because you think that by them you possess eternal life. These are the Scriptures that testify about me, yet you refuse to come to me to have life.
9. Joshua 5:13–14 Now when Joshua was near Jericho, he looked up and saw a man standing in front of him with a drawn sword in his hand. Joshua went up to him and asked, "Are you for us or for our enemies?" "Neither," he replied, "but as commander of the army of the Lord I have now come." Then Joshua fell facedown to the ground in reverence, and asked him, "What message does my Lord have for his servant?"

10. Ephesians 6:17 Take the helmet of salvation and the sword of the Spirit, which is the word of God.
11. Proverbs 16:2 All a man's ways seem innocent to him, but motives are weighed by the Lord.
12. 1 John 2:27 As for you, the anointing you received from him remains in you, and you do not need anyone to teach you. But as his anointing teaches you about all things and as that anointing is real, not counterfeit—just as it has taught you, remain in him.
    2 Corinthians 3:3 You show that you are a letter from Christ, the result of our ministry, written not with ink but with the Spirit of the living God, not on tablets of stone but on tablets of human hearts.
13. Luke 9:23 Then he said to them all: "If anyone would come after me, he must deny himself and take up his cross daily and follow me."
14. John 12:49 For I did not speak of my own accord, but the Father who sent me commanded me what to say and how to say it.
15. Proverbs 18:2 A fool finds no pleasure in understanding but delights in airing his own opinions.

Chapter 5: Growing Up

1. Luke 5:8 When Simon Peter saw this, he fell at Jesus' knees and said, "Go away from me, Lord; I am a sinful man!"
2. Galatians 4:19 My dear children, for whom I am again in the pains of childbirth until Christ is formed in you,
3. Romans 12:3 For by the grace given me I say to every one of you: Do not think of yourself more highly than you ought, but rather think of yourself with sober judgment, in accordance with the measure of faith God has given you.
4. James 1:19 My dear brothers, take note of this: Everyone should be quick to listen, slow to speak and slow to become angry,
5. Hebrews 5:14 But solid food is for the mature, who by constant use have trained themselves to distinguish good from evil.

Chapter 6: The Need for Self Crucified

1. Mark 6:5–6 He could not do any miracles there, except lay his hands on a few sick people and heal them. And he was amazed at their lack of faith. Then Jesus went around teaching from village to village.

2. John 12:25 The man who loves his life will lose it, while the man who hates his life in this world will keep it for eternal life.
3. *Even the Demons Believe,* by Timothy Williams, ISBN 1-57921-355-3

Chapter 7: The Shame of the Cross

1. Philippians 3:6 as for zeal, persecuting the church; as for legalistic righteousness, faultless.
2. Acts 26:11 Many a time I went from one synagogue to another to have them punished, and I tried to force them to blaspheme. In my obsession against them, I even went to foreign cities to persecute them.
3. 1 Timothy 1:13 Even though I was once a blasphemer and a persecutor and a violent man, I was shown mercy because I acted in ignorance and unbelief.
4. Acts 26:14 We all fell to the ground, and I heard a voice saying to me in Aramaic, "Saul, Saul, why do you persecute me? It is hard for you to kick against the goads." [Goads are God's small comments where He is trying to get us to move in a certain direction.]
5. Ephesians 4:8–15 This is why it says: "When he ascended on high, he led captives in his train and gave gifts to men." (What does "he ascended" mean except that he also descended to the lower, earthly regions? He who descended is the very one who ascended higher than all the heavens, in order to fill the whole universe.) It was he who gave some to be apostles, some to be prophets, some to be evangelists, and some to be pastors and teachers, to prepare God's people for works of service, so that the body of Christ may be built up until we all reach unity in the faith and in the knowledge of the Son of God and become mature, attaining to the whole measure of the fullness of Christ. Then we will no longer be infants, tossed back and forth by the waves, and blown here and there by every wind of teaching and by the cunning and craftiness of men in their deceitful scheming. Instead, speaking the truth in love, we will in all things grow up into him who is the Head, that is, Christ.
6. Psalm 42:7 Deep calls to deep in the roar of your waterfalls; all your waves and breakers have swept over me.

Chapter 8: Teenage Years

1. Philippians 2:12 Therefore, my dear friends, as you have always obeyed—not only in my presence, but now much more in my absence—continue to work out your salvation with fear and trembling,
2. Galatians 5:17 For the sinful nature desires what is contrary to the Spirit, and the Spirit what is contrary to the sinful nature. They are in conflict with each other, so that you do not do what you want.
3. Galatians 2:20 I have been crucified with Christ and I no longer live, but Christ lives in me. The life I live in the body, I live by faith in the Son of God, who loved me and gave himself for me.
4. Psalm 37:4 Delight yourself in the Lord and he will give you the desires of your heart.
5. Romans 8:23 Not only so, but we ourselves, who have the firstfruits of the Spirit, groan inwardly as we wait eagerly for our adoption as sons, the redemption of our bodies.
6. John 12:26 Whoever serves me must follow me; and where I am, my servant also will be. My Father will honor the one who serves me.

Chapter 9: God's Paths, Commands, Precepts, Ways, and Laws

1. Matthew 15:12, Matthew 17:27, John 7:1, Luke 13:31–32, Matthew 23, John 8:11
2. John 3:8 The wind blows wherever it pleases. You hear its sound, but you cannot tell where it comes from or where it is going. So it is with everyone born of the Spirit.
3. Lamentations 3:25–28 The Lord is good to those whose hope is in him, to the one who seeks him; it is good to wait quietly for the salvation of the Lord. It is good for a man to bear the yoke while he is young. Let him sit alone in silence, for the Lord has laid it on him.
4. Colossians 2:6 So then, just as you received Christ Jesus as Lord, continue to live in him,
5. Hebrews 6:7–8 Land that drinks in the rain often falling on it and that produces a crop useful to those for whom it is farmed receives the blessing of God. But land that produces thorns and thistles is worthless and is in danger of being cursed. In the end it will be burned.

6. Matthew 24:45 Who then is the faithful and wise servant, whom the master has put in charge of the servants in his household to give them their food at the proper time?
7. Psalm 131:1–2 A song of ascents. Of David. My heart is not proud, O Lord, my eyes are not haughty; I do not concern myself with great matters or things too wonderful for me. But I have stilled and quieted my soul; like a weaned child with its mother, like a weaned child is my soul within me.
8. John 4:23 Yet a time is coming and has now come when the true worshipers will worship the Father in spirit and truth, for they are the kind of worshipers the Father seeks.
9. Ezekiel 13:10–12 Because they lead my people astray, saying, "Peace," when there is no peace, and because, when a flimsy wall is built, they cover it with whitewash, therefore tell those who cover it with whitewash that it is going to fall. Rain will come in torrents, and I will send hailstones hurtling down, and violent winds will burst forth. When the wall collapses, will people not ask you, "Where is the whitewash you covered it with?"
10. 1 Peter 1:13 Therefore, prepare your minds for action; be self-controlled; set your hope fully on the grace to be given you when Jesus Christ is revealed.
11. Colossians 3:2 Set your minds on things above, not on earthly things.

Chapter 10: Dreams, Visions, and Spiritual Gifts

1. Acts 5:32 We are witnesses of these things, and so is the Holy Spirit, whom God has given to those who obey him.
2. Ecclesiastes 5:3 As a dream comes when there are many cares, so the speech of a fool when there are many words.
3. Jeremiah 23:16 This is what the Lord Almighty says: "Do not listen to what the prophets are prophesying to you; they fill you with false hopes. They speak visions from their own minds, not from the mouth of the Lord."
4. Psalm 27:8 My heart says of you, "Seek his face!" Your face, Lord, I will seek.
5. John 6:26 Jesus answered, "I tell you the truth, you are looking for me, not because you saw miraculous signs but because you ate the loaves and had your fill."
   Revelation 22:3–4 No longer will there be any curse. The throne of God and of the Lamb will be in the city, and his servants will serve him. They will see his face, and his name will be on their foreheads.

6. 1 Kings 22:22 "By what means?" the Lord asked. "I will go out and be a lying spirit in the mouths of all his prophets," he said. "You will succeed in enticing him," said the Lord. "Go and do it."
7. 1 Thessalonians 5:20 do not treat prophecies with contempt. Acts 21:10–11 After we had been there a number of days, a prophet named Agabus came down from Judea. Coming over to us, he took Paul's belt, tied his own hands and feet with it and said, "The Holy Spirit says, 'In this way the Jews of Jerusalem will bind the owner of this belt and will hand him over to the Gentiles.'"

Chapter 11: God's Voice and Unity

1. Psalm 133 A song of ascents. Of David. How good and pleasant it is when brothers live together in unity! It is like precious oil poured on the head, running down on the beard, running down on Aaron's beard, down upon the collar of his robes. It is as if the dew of Hermon were falling on Mount Zion. For there the Lord bestows his blessing, even life forevermore.
2. Jeremiah 23:30 "Therefore," declares the Lord, "I am against the prophets who steal from one another words supposedly from me."
3. Galatians 2:11 When Peter came to Antioch, I opposed him to his face, because he was clearly in the wrong.

Chapter 12: How to Hear God Through Others

1. 1 John 1:9 If we confess our sins, he is faithful and just and will forgive us our sins and purify us from all unrighteousness.
2. 2 Corinthians 11:26b . . . and in danger from false brothers.
3. Of course many speak of getting a bad feeling about the message of the cross. That is the flesh and the Evil One trying to keep them from the Truth.
4. 1 Thessalonians 2:10 You are witnesses, and so is God, of how holy, righteous and blameless we were among you who believed.

Chapter 13: When God Is Silent

1. John 8:24 I told you that you would die in your sins; if you do not believe that I am the one I claim to be, you will indeed die in your sins. [Believing who Jesus is, means that we believe that just as He was one with the Father, Jesus came to bring that same relationship.]
2. 2 Corinthians 11:14 And no wonder, for Satan himself masquerades as an angel of light.

3. Genesis 3:8 Then the man and his wife heard the sound of the Lord God as he was walking in the garden in the cool of the day, and they hid from the Lord God among the trees of the garden.
4. Hebrews 6:3 And God permitting, we will do so.
5. Psalm 84:7 They go from strength to strength, till each appears before God in Zion.
6. Genesis 3:9 But the Lord God called to the man, "Where are you?"
7. 2 Kings 20:12–13 At that time Merodach-Baladan son of Baladan king of Babylon sent Hezekiah letters and a gift, because he had heard of Hezekiah's illness. Hezekiah received the messengers and showed them all that was in his storehouses—the silver, the gold, the spices and the fine oil—his armory and everything found among his treasures. There was nothing in his palace or in all his kingdom that Hezekiah did not show them.
8. Psalm 127:1–2 A song of ascents. Of Solomon. Unless the Lord builds the house, its builders labor in vain. Unless the Lord watches over the city, the watchmen stand guard in vain. In vain you rise early and stay up late, toiling for food to eat—for he grants sleep to those he loves.
9. John 3:34 For the one whom God has sent speaks the words of God, for God gives the Spirit without limit.
10. James 3:2 We all stumble in many ways. If anyone is never at fault in what he says, he is a perfect man, able to keep his whole body in check.
11. Hebrews 12:11 No discipline seems pleasant at the time, but painful. Later on, however, it produces a harvest of righteousness and peace for those who have been trained by it.
12. 1 Corinthians 10:11 These things happened to them as examples and were written down as warnings for us, on whom the fulfillment of the ages has come.
13. Exodus 15:22–26 Then Moses led Israel from the Red Sea and they went into the Desert of Shur. For three days they traveled in the desert without finding water. When they came to Marah, they could not drink its water because it was bitter. (That is why the place is called Marah.) So the people grumbled against Moses, saying, "What are we to drink?" Then Moses cried out to the Lord, and the Lord showed him a piece of wood. He threw it into the water, and the water became sweet. There the Lord made a decree and a law for them, and there he tested them. He said, "If you listen carefully to the voice of the Lord your God and do what is

right in his eyes, if you pay attention to his commands and keep all his decrees, I will not bring on you any of the diseases I brought on the Egyptians, for I am the Lord, who heals you."

14. John 6:26 Jesus answered, "I tell you the truth, you are looking for me, not because you saw miraculous signs but because you ate the loaves and had your fill."

Chapter 14: The Facial Expressions of God

1. 1 Corinthians 13:12 Now we see but a poor reflection as in a mirror; then we shall see face to face. Now I know in part; then I shall know fully, even as I am fully known.
   1 John 3:2 Dear friends, now we are children of God, and what we will be has not yet been made known. But we know that when he appears, we shall be like him, for we shall see him as he is.

Chapter 15: Adulthood—The Spirit of Pentecost

1. Romans 8:17 Now if we are children, then we are heirs—heirs of God and co-heirs with Christ, if indeed we share in his sufferings in order that we may also share in his glory.
2. John 20:21–23 Again Jesus said, "Peace be with you! As the Father has sent me, I am sending you." And with that he breathed on them and said, "Receive the Holy Spirit. If you forgive anyone his sins, they are forgiven; if you do not forgive them, they are not forgiven."
3. Galatians 2:20 I have been crucified with Christ and I no longer live, but Christ lives in me. The life I live in the body, I live by faith in the Son of God, who loved me and gave himself for me.
   John 20:22–23 And with that he breathed on them and said, "Receive the Holy Spirit. If you forgive anyone his sins, they are forgiven; if you do not forgive them, they are not forgiven."
4. Romans 9:3 For I could wish that I myself were cursed and cut off from Christ for the sake of my brothers, those of my own race,
5. John 12:27 Now my heart is troubled, and what shall I say? "Father, save me from this hour"? No, it was for this very reason I came to this hour. [Let us not pray that God deliver us from our hour of suffering, but rather, that we might be faithful in that hour.]

Chapter 16: Judgment and Judging

1. [So dead was John to himself that he was able to test for a lie or for truth by the mere fact if someone listened to what he had to say.] 1 John 4:6 We are from God, and whoever knows God listens to us; but whoever is not from God does not listen to us. This is how we recognize the Spirit of truth and the spirit of falsehood.
2. 1 Corinthians 2:15 The spiritual man makes judgments about all things, but he himself is not subject to any man's judgment:
3. 1 Thessalonians 4:11 Make it your ambition to lead a quiet life, to mind your own business and to work with your hands, just as we told you,
4. 1 Corinthians 4:5 Therefore judge nothing before the appointed time; wait till the Lord comes. He will bring to light what is hidden in darkness and will expose the motives of men's hearts. At that time each will receive his praise from God.
5. Matthew 7:1 Do not judge, or you too will be judged.

Chapter 17: God's Voice and Conviction of Sin

1. Romans 3:12 All have turned away, they have together become worthless; there is no one who does good, not even one.
2. Hebrews 4:12 For the word of God is living and active. Sharper than any double-edged sword, it penetrates even to dividing soul and spirit, joints and marrow; it judges the thoughts and attitudes of the heart.
3. 1 Corinthians 12:3 Therefore I tell you that no one who is speaking by the Spirit of God says, "Jesus be cursed," and no one can say, "Jesus is Lord," except by the Holy Spirit.
4. John 14:26 But the Counselor, the Holy Spirit, whom the Father will send in my name, will teach you all things and will remind you of everything I have said to you.

Chapter 18: The Fruit of Old Age

1. Hebrews 11:13 All these people were still living by faith when they died. They did not receive the things promised; they only saw them and welcomed them from a distance. And they admitted that they were aliens and strangers on earth.
2. 2 Peter 3:14 So then, dear friends, since you are looking forward to this, make every effort to be found spotless, blameless and at peace with him.

3. Numbers 14:44 Nevertheless, in their presumption they went up toward the high hill country, though neither Moses nor the ark of the Lord's covenant moved from the camp.
4. John 12:26 Whoever serves me must follow me; and where I am, my servant also will be. My Father will honor the one who serves me.
5. Acts 7:56–58 "Look," he said, "I see heaven open and the Son of Man standing at the right hand of God." At this they covered their ears and, yelling at the top of their voices, they all rushed at him, dragged him out of the city and began to stone him. Meanwhile, the witnesses laid their clothes at the feet of a young man named Saul.
6. 1 Corinthians 10:13 No temptation has seized you except what is common to man. And God is faithful; he will not let you be tempted beyond what you can bear. But when you are tempted, he will also provide a way out so that you can stand up under it.
7. 2 Thessalonians 2:14 He called you to this through our gospel, that you might share in the glory of our Lord Jesus Christ.
8. Acts 9:31 Then the church throughout Judea, Galilee and Samaria enjoyed a time of peace. It was strengthened; and encouraged by the Holy Spirit, it grew in numbers, living in the fear of the Lord.
9. Acts 3:26 When God raised up his servant, he sent him first to you to bless you by turning each of you from your wicked ways.
10. Romans 8:16 The Spirit himself testifies with our spirit that we are God's children.
11. Psalm 29:5 The voice of the Lord breaks the cedars; the Lord breaks in pieces the cedars of Lebanon.

Chapter 19: First Step—Laying a Foundation

1. 1 Corinthians 4:13 when we are slandered, we answer kindly. Up to this moment we have become the scum of the earth, the refuse of the world.
2. 1 Corinthians 6:13 "Food for the stomach and the stomach for food"—but God will destroy them both. The body is not meant for sexual immorality, but for the Lord, and the Lord for the body.

Chapter 20: Cord of Three—A Summary

1. 1 Corinthians 3:15 If it is burned up, he will suffer loss; he himself will be saved, but only as one escaping through the flames.
2. Galatians 4:9a But now that you know God—or rather are known by God . . .
3. Colossians 2:23 Such regulations indeed have an appearance of wisdom, with their self-imposed worship, their false humility and their harsh treatment of the body, but they lack any value in restraining sensual indulgence.
4. [By this we do not mean treating the flesh harshly. Rather, one must follow Jesus and deny self only to the measure and by the means that God is providing at the time.] Colossians 2:23 Such regulations indeed have an appearance of wisdom, with their self-imposed worship, their false humility and their harsh treatment of the body, but they lack any value in restraining sensual indulgence.
5. 2 Corinthians 1:5 For just as the sufferings of Christ flow over into our lives, so also through Christ our comfort overflows.
6. 2 Corinthians 6:10 sorrowful, yet always rejoicing; poor, yet making many rich; having nothing, and yet possessing everything.
7. 2 Corinthians 4:10 We always carry around in our body the death of Jesus, so that the life of Jesus may also be revealed in our body.
8. Mark 8:34 Then he called the crowd to him along with his disciples and said: "If anyone would come after me, he must deny himself and take up his cross and follow me."

Other Books by Timothy Williams

Even the Demons Believe

- A small book that details how to get started in the new life of Christ.
  ISBN 1-57921-355-3

Insanity in the Church

- Exposes the errors of loving self that are in the church and introduces the solution.
  ISBN 1-57921-390-1

Whisper Revival

- How to prepare yourself for revival when God moves, as well as what dangers to look for.
  ISBN 1-57921-274-3

101 Ways to Deny Self

- This book is based on 1 Peter 1:13 where we are called to prepare our minds for action. It is not a list of rules,

but a preparation for the Holy Spirit to guide us in joyful obedience.
ISBN 1-57921-397-9

Hating for Jesus (John 12:25)

- A very hard hitting, detailed book about the offensive message of the cross. It is a difficult read and one will have to persevere to get through it. If the reader does, rich joy will be found.
ISBN 1-57921-646-3

eau de Cult – The Fragrance of Love in the First Church

- This book explains the fruit of God's love being worked in a body of believers and how many will consider that to look like a cult.
ISBN 1-57921-511-4

Bewitchment – The Foolish Galatians

- While this book is written to a specific denomination it really is a call to all of us to be sure we are walking in the Spirit and not human effort.
ISBN 1-57921-469-X

Prosperity Teachers

- This book reveals how and when God gives us the desires of our hearts. It will cause you to carefully examine what the Bible teaches on prosperity.
ISBN 1-57921-489-4

Bad Fruit

- This book examines both sides of the "once saved, always saved" debate and discusses the fruit produced in the lives of those who believe they can never fall from grace.
Soft cover: ISBN 1-57921-556-4
Hard cover: ISBN 1-57921-638-2

To order additional copies of

EARS TO HEAR

call

Toll free: (877) 421-READ (7323)

Printed in the United States
17654LVS00001B/374